I0475927

Tarpits & Abstraction

Matt Neary

Contents

Chapter 1

Computation

Computation is the evaluation of a given expression, usually by means of computer. For example, one could compute the addition $3 + 5$ and arrive at 8. With a few basic operators and a number system, the entirety of arithmetic is computable; however, there are more complex structures which cannot be discussed under these limitations.

For the sake of working with more complex structures, we rely upon *abstraction*. Let's look at an example. You have undoubtedly seen an expression like the following in a mathematical setting.

Figure 1.1:

$$f(x) \ = \ x^2$$

The object $f(x)$ is more complex than primitive operators and numbers because it accepts argument to its computation. Objects like this one are formed by a process known as abstraction. Along with abstraction, the other fundamental aspects of computation are *variables* and *application*. A variable is a given token within an expression intended for substitution, and application is the reduction of an expression from an abstracted form. Here are some more concrete examples.

In Figure 1.2, we have the abstraction of the expression x^2 in which x is a variable. We then apply $f(x)$ to 3.

Figure 1.2:

$$f(x) = x^2$$
$$y = f(3) \implies y = 9$$

1.1   A Foundational Grammar

We have discussed the features necessary for a langauge to facilli-
tate computation; however, we have so far relied upon the familiar
notation of mathematics. We will now switch to a language defined
specifically as a foundation for computation. The Lambda Calculus
is a language consisting of variables, abstraction, and application.
The notation can be summarized by the Backus-Naur definition in
Figure 1.3.

Figure 1.3:

$< expr >$ $::= \lambda < var > < expr >$
                    $| (< expr >) < expr >$
                    $| < var >$

BNF is perfect for the description of languages, both expressive
and formal. In describing the Lambda Calculus, an expression
(*expr*) is said to be one of three forms. The first form is a lambda
followed by a variable, its argument, and finally followed by another
expression. The next is simply the application of one expression to
another, and the last is simpe variable reference.

These are the only forms, a data-type like numbers is not provided. However, we will for now take its potential to represent such
data as granted. Let's explore this notation.

The expression in Figure 1.4 defines an identity function and
then applies it to the number 3. The result, of course, is 3.

In the notation of traditional math, we would have defined this
function prior to its invocation. Such a form would appear as in
Figure 1.5 and achieve the behavior of Figure 1.4.

The Lambda Calculus is a fully-versatile language; however, it

Figure 1.4:

$$(\lambda\ x\ x)3$$

Figure 1.5:

$$f(x)\ =\ x$$
$$f(3)$$

is what some describe as a *Turing tarpit*. Alan Perlis describes a Turing tarpit as a language "in which everything is possible but nothing of interest is easy." Despite this nature of the Lambda Calculus, we will be forming quite complex programs throughout this book on its foundation. We will, in a sense, climb out of its tarpit by means of abstraction. In order to do so, we will build up a scaffolding of abstraction, building layer upon layer as we construct an edifice of procedures.

1.2 A Symbolic Language

In the previous section, we utilized numbers within the Lambda Calculus; however, we do not accept them as primitive. Rather, we will need to define them in terms of the Lambda Calculus. Of course, the ability to refer to numbers by name would be helpful. For this reason, amongst many others, we will begin by defining a new, symbolic language on top of the Lambda Calculus, adding a layer of abstraction to our computation.

Our layer of abstraction will be a uniform language of Symbolic Expressions which is a dialect of the language called Lisp. These symbolic expressions are parentheses enclosed arrays of symbols, taking on different meanings based on their matching of patterns which we will define.

Figure 1.6 displays an example.

The expression in Figure 1.6 evaluates to 5. In this case our expression is a function application receiving two numbers as arguments. This syntax is very simple, uniform and legible. Addition-

Figure 1.6:

(+ 2 3)

ally, as you will see later on in this book, it is very easily interpreted by program.

1.3 Symbolic Expressions

The language into which we are entering is one of symbolic expressions. All of our expressions will take the form defined by the grammar in Figure 1.7. This uniformity will make its definition in terms of Lambda Calculus far easier, and simplify its later interpretation or compilation.

Figure 1.7:

$< expr >$	$::= < sexpr > \mid < atom >$
$< sexpr >$	$::= (< list >)$
$< list >$	$::= < expr > \mid < expr > < expr >$

1.4 Defining Semantics

1.4.1 Primitive Forms

Now, these Symbolic Expressions or *S-Expressions* can take any of a multitude of forms. Of these, we will define meaning for forms of interesting patterns. We begin, unsurprisingly, with an S-Expression which serves to create lambdas. All forms matching the patterns which we discuss will be converted to the provided form, labeled as the consequent.

Essentially, we are saying that any expression of the given form should be a function of the provided arguments bearing the provided expression.

Figure 1.8:

$$(lambda\ (var)\ expr) \qquad\qquad \Longrightarrow \quad \lambda var\ expr$$
$$(lambda\ (var\ rest\ldots)\ expr) \quad \Longrightarrow \quad \lambda var\ (lambda\ rest\ expr)$$

Additionally, we provide a default case for our S-Expressions. Should certain expression match none of our provided patterns, we will default to function invocation. In other words, in Figure 1.9 we define a pattern for those values which match no other patterns.

Figure 1.9:

$$(fn\ val) \qquad\qquad = (fn)val$$
$$(fn\ val\ rest\ldots) \qquad = ((fn)val\ rest)$$

The Lambda Calculus has now been fully implemented in our symbolic forms; however, we will add many more features for the sake of convenience. After all, our goal was to add abstraction, not move a few symbols around!

1.4.2 Evaluation of Symbolic Forms

Before we continue, we'll look at some examples of our syntax as implemented so far. In evaluating a Lambda Calculus expression, or in this case, derived form, the single operation necessary is known as reduction. Reduction is conversion of an expression of function application to a new expression, one derived by substitution of the argument value.

To begin gaining familiarity with our language, we look at a function of two variables. The function in Figure 1.10 performs f on a value x, and then f once more on the resultant value.

Now we will look at a similar form, a function of three variables. In Figure 1.11 is a function of values g, f, and x. The result is similar to that of the one in Figure 1.10, but this time replacing (fx) with (gfx).

So far we have covered some examples of Symbolic Expressions,

Figure 1.10:

$$(lambda\ (f\ x)\ (f\ (f\ x)))$$

Figure 1.11:

$$(lambda\ (g\ f\ x)\ (f\ (g\ f\ x)))$$

but all of them have been of the lambda definition form. Furthermore, they have lacked any concrete meaning. To explore the additional notation we have defined, we will apply the former expression to the latter, which expands into Figure 1.12.

Figure 1.12:

$$((lambda\ (g\ f\ x)\ (f\ (g\ f\ x)))\ (lambda\ (f\ x)\ (f\ (f\ x))))$$

This expression appears quite complex, so let's use the aforementioned reduction operation to simplify it. Recall from our definition of *lambda* that a function of multiple variables evaluated for one results in a function of one-less variable than the initial form. Hence we begin by substituting our argument for g throughout the expression; later steps are of a similar nature.

That looks much better! What we have arrived at is only slightly different than our initial function of f and x. The only change was the number of times that f was applied. We have explored the reduction of a symbolic expression to a result; however, this result is far from tangible.

In order for computation by means of the Lambda Calculus to render a human-readable result, we will need a notation of expression exhibited by function definitions. That means that, for example, the function $(lambda\ (a)\ (a\ (a\ (a\ a))))$ could serve to communicate the number four.

The expressive power of this notation is clear; however, appli-

Figure 1.13:

$$((lambda\ (g\ f\ x)\ (f\ (g\ f\ x)))\ (lambda\ (f\ x)\ (f\ (f\ x))))$$
$$\Longrightarrow \quad (lambda\ (f\ x)\ (f\ ((lambda\ (f\ x)\ (f\ (f\ x)))\ f\ x)))$$
$$\Longrightarrow \quad (lambda\ (f\ x)\ (f\ (f\ (f\ x))))$$

cation of a function to itself as in (aa) is very rarely appropriate, and so we will slightly expand our expression of four to serve a more concrete purpose within the language. We now expand our numeric function representing some number n to accept two parameters, and return the application of the first parameter n times to the second parameter. Hence, the number four would look like the function in Figure 1.14.

Figure 1.14:

$$(lambda\ (f\ n)\ (f\ (f\ (f\ (f\ n)))))$$

This notation, of course, translates just as well into an expression of any number. The number three would look like the function in Figure 1.15.

Figure 1.15:

$$(lambda\ (f\ n)\ (f\ (f\ (f\ n))))$$

Hopefully these examples have given you a feel for how this syntax can work, and maybe even an early sense of how useful functions will emerge from the Lambda Calculus.

1.5   Foundations in Lambda Calculus

To accompany our syntactic constructs, we will need to define some forms in the Lambda Calculus, especially data-types and their ma-

nipulations. Our definitions will be illustrated as equalities, like
$id = \lambda x x$; however, syntactic patterns will be expressed as impli-
cations. Recall that in Lambda Calculus there are only functions,
no literals or primitive data-types. To combat this apparent short-
coming of the language, we will need to give data-types of interest a
functional form. The examples of the prior section were a preview
into how our conceptualization of numbers will behave.

1.5.1   Numbers

Numbers are a rather fundamental data-type, especially in modern
computing. Additionally, they are in most other languages seen as
atomic and primitive. However, we must provide a definition for
the behavior of numbers in our language constituent of functions.
We begin with a means of defining all natural numbers inductively,
via the successor.

Figure 1.16:

$$0 = \lambda f \lambda x\, x$$
$$succ = \lambda n \lambda f \lambda x\, (f)((n)f)x$$

Our definition of numbers is just like the examples from the
previous section. Notice that 1, for example, could be easily defined as $1 = (succ\ 0)$, as could any positive integer with enough
applications of $succ$. Later on when we return to syntactic features
we will define all numbers in this way; the numbers will take on
their usual form as a string of decimal digits.

Numbers are our first data-type. Their definition is iterative
in nature, with zero meaning no applications of the function f to
x. We now will define some elementary manipulations of this data-
type, i.e., basic arithmetic. The definitions in Figure 1.17 are pretty
straightforward; nearly all of them consist exclusively of iterative
application of a more primitive function to a base value.

Addition merely takes advantage of the iterative nature of our
numbers to apply the successor n times, starting with m. In a
similar manner, multiplication applies addition repeatedly starting
with zero. The predecessor is much more complicated, so let's work
our way through its evaluation.

Figure 1.17:

$$+ \qquad\qquad\qquad\qquad\quad = \lambda\, n\, \lambda\, m\, ((n)succ)m$$
$$* \qquad\qquad\qquad\qquad\quad = \lambda\, n\, \lambda\, m\, ((n)(sum)m)0$$
$$pred \quad = \lambda\, n\, \lambda\, f\, \lambda\, z\, ((((n)\,\lambda\, g\, \lambda\, h\, (h)(g)f)\lambda\, u\, z)\lambda\, u\, u)$$
$$- \qquad\qquad\qquad\qquad\quad = \lambda\, n\, \lambda\, m\, ((m)pred)n$$

We'll begin our exploration of the *pred* function by looking at the value of two. Since two equals $(succ)(succ)0$ we can work out its Lambda form, or simply take as a given that is the function in Figure 1.18.

Figure 1.18:

$$2 \;=\; \lambda\, f\, \lambda\, x\, (f)(f)x$$

Now we can evaluate *pred* for this value. *pred* has been defined already, but let's briefly render it in the more succinct form of Figure 1.19. The form in Figure 1.19 is very easily translated back to Lambda Calculus and should serve to cut through at least a portion of the complexity of the definition.

Figure 1.19:

$$pred \;=\; \lambda\, n\, \lambda\, f\, \lambda\, z\, ((\lambda\, g\, \lambda\, h\, (h)(g)f)^{n}\, \lambda\, u\, z)\, \lambda\, u\, u$$

With the rendering of the definition displayed in Figure 1.19 in mind, we aim to reduce an application of *pred* to 2 to a result.

Now that we have reduced the expression to the form of our prior rendering of *pred*, we expand it into a true Lambda Calculus form, as seen in Figure 1.21 and continue our reduction.

In the conversions of Figure 1.22, as in all, our reductions will need to take place in a right-to-left direction when evaluating expressions of the form $(f)(g)x$. Recall that our goal here is to reduce

Figure 1.20:

$$(\lambda\, n\, \lambda\, f\, \lambda\, z\, ((\lambda\, g\, \lambda\, h\, (h)(g)f)^{n}\, \lambda\, u\, z)\, \lambda\, u\, u)\, 2$$
$$(\lambda\, f\, \lambda\, z\, ((\lambda\, g\, \lambda\, h\, (h)(g)f)^{2}\, \lambda\, u\, z)\, \lambda\, u\, u)$$

Figure 1.21:

$$(\lambda\, f\, \lambda\, z\, (((\lambda\, g\, \lambda\, h\, (h)(g)f)\, (\lambda\, g\, \lambda\, h\, (h)(g)f))\, \lambda\, u\, z)\, \lambda\, u\, u)$$

a complex form to simplistic result, and we have already made significant progress.

Figure 1.22:

$$(\lambda\, f\, \lambda\, z\, ((\lambda\, g\, \lambda\, h\, (h)(g)f)\, (\lambda\, h\, (h)(\lambda\, u\, z)f))\, \lambda\, u\, u)$$
$$(\lambda\, f\, \lambda\, z\, ((\lambda\, g\, \lambda\, h\, (h)(g)f)\, (\lambda\, h\, (h)z))\, \lambda\, u\, u)$$
$$(\lambda\, f\, \lambda\, z\, (\lambda\, h\, (h)(\lambda\, h\, (h)z)f)\, \lambda\, u\, u)$$
$$(\lambda\, f\, \lambda\, z\, (\lambda\, h\, (h)(f)z)\, \lambda\, u\, u)$$

The forms in Figure 1.22 were all mere substitutions, as should be expected. If any were unclear, try working those steps out in a notebook. We are now finally ready to reduce the application of the identity (*lambda u u*) and achieve our final result.

Our result, seen in Figure 1.23 was a single application of f to z, i.e., one. Hence you have seen that at least in this case, the *pred* function did its job. Achieving an intuitive grasp of how it works is unfortunately not as straight-forward. If you wish to, keep in mind that $\lambda u z$ maps a value to the numeric starting point, and $\lambda u u$ leaves an expression alone. So the decrement occurs by the setting of the origin later than it would normally occur.

With our complex definition of the predecessor complete, subtraction is trivial. Once again we perform an iterative process on a base value, this time that process is *pred*.

Figure 1.23:

$$\lambda f \, \lambda \, z \, (\lambda \, u \, u)(f)z$$
$$\lambda f \, \lambda \, z \, (f)z$$

1.5.2 Booleans

Having defined numbers and their manipulations, we will work on booleans. Booleans are the values of true and false, or in our syntax, t and f. Booleans are quite necessary in expressing conditional statements; thus we provide the concomitant *if* function. These values will give us great power in their ability to branch results to a function, in a sense constructing piece-wise functions. It is by this ability that we are able to form a multitude of inductive definitions, as well as other important forms.

Figure 1.24:

$$\#t \qquad\qquad = \lambda \, a \, \lambda \, b \, (a)id$$
$$\#f \qquad\qquad = \lambda \, a \, \lambda \, b \, (b)id$$
$$if \qquad\qquad = \lambda \, p \, \lambda \, t \, \lambda \, f \, ((p)\lambda \, \_ \, t)\lambda \, \_ \, f$$

The key to our booleans is that they accept two functions as parameters, functions that serve to encapsulate values, of which one will be chosen. Once chosen, that function is executed with the arbitrarily-chosen identity as an argument. This method of wrapping the decision serves as a means of lazy evaluation, and is fully realized in the lambda-underscores wrapping the branches of an *if* statement.

Now, since of course no boolean system is complete without some boolean algebra, we define *and* and *or*. These functions perform the operations you would expect; $(andab)$ is true only when both a and b are true, but $(orab)$ is true if either argument is true. Their definitions follow easily from our *if* function. Keep in mind that both of these functions operate only on booleans.

With boolean manipulation and conditionals in hand, we need

Figure 1.25:

$$and \qquad\qquad = \lambda\, a\, \lambda\, b\, (((if)a)b)\#f$$
$$or \qquad\qquad = \lambda\, a\, \lambda\, b\, (((if)a)\#t)b$$

some useful predicates to utilize them. We define some basic predicates on numbers in Figure 1.26. *eq* will be very useful in later developments; it is one of McCarthy's elementary functions.

Figure 1.26:

$$zero? \qquad\qquad = \lambda\, n\, ((n)x\#f)\#t$$
$$leq \qquad\qquad = \lambda\, a\, \lambda\, b\, (zero?)((-)m)n$$
$$eq \qquad\qquad = \lambda\, a\, \lambda\, b\, (and\ (leq\ a\ b)\ (leq\ b\ a))$$

The predicates in Figure 1.26 serve to identify traits of a given number or given numbers. *zero?* is true when a number is zero, *leq* is true when the first number is less than or equal to the second, and *eq* determines whether two numbers are equal.

1.5.3   Pairs

Finally we reach the most important part of our S-Expressions, their underlying lists. That is to say, every Symbolic Expression is innately a list of other expressions, whether atomic or symbolic, and these lists serve as an analog to a the list data-type. To construct lists we will opt for a sort of linked-list implementation in our lambda definitions. We begin with a pair and a *nil* definition, each readily revealing their type by opting for either the passed *c* or *n* function. The function definitions are displayed in Figure 1.27.

cons constructs a pair when given two values, and accepts a function which will receive the two items to manipulate. *nil* on the other hand serves as a sort of empty pair, and instead fires the second provided function to identify itself as such.

Now, once again we follow a defined data-type with its manipulations. Just as did McCarthy, we will provide *car* and *cdr* as

Figure 1.27:

$$
\begin{aligned}
cons &= \lambda\,a\,\lambda\,b\,\lambda\,c\,\lambda\,n\;((c)a)b \\
nil &= \lambda\,c\,\lambda\,n\;(n)id
\end{aligned}
$$

additional elementary functions, with *pair?* and *null?* serving as complements to each other in determining the end of a list. *car* returns the first value of a pair, and *cdr* the second. Their names are quite historical and refer to address access of a pair in memory, but you can just think of them as /kαr/ and /kuder/.

Figure 1.28:

$$
\begin{aligned}
car &= \lambda\,l\;(((l)\lambda\,a\,\lambda\,b\,a)id) \\
cdr &= \lambda\,l\;(((l)\lambda\,a\,\lambda\,b\,b)id) \\
pair? &= \lambda\,l\;(((l)\lambda\,\_\,\lambda\,\_\,\#t)\lambda\,\_\,\#f) \\
null? &= \lambda\,l\;(((l)\lambda\,\_\,\lambda\,\_\,\#f)\lambda\,\_\,\#t)
\end{aligned}
$$

car provides that pair with a pair handling function that returns the first element, and an arbitrary *nil* handling function. Similarly, *cdr* provides a pair handling function returning the second element. *pair?* and *null?* are logical opposites to each other, each provides a pair- and nil-handling function, returning either t or f as is appropriate.

Together, these functions are sufficient for designing a list implementation. The implementation that comes naturally is known as a linked-list. A linked-list is essentially either a pair of an element and a linked-list or *nil*. If that is unclear, think of a tree with a fractal structure. The tree consists of a leaf and a child tree, which in turn has both leaf and child tree, until the tree ends with *nil* for a child tree.

1.5.4 Recursion

Our last definition will be a bit more esoteric, or at least complex. We define a *Y Combinator*. This function, Y, will allow another to be executed accepting itself as an argument. The Y Combinator refers to a specific combinator, but you have already seen another. The *I* Combinator is defined as $\lambda x x$ in the Lambda Calculus. The key to combinators is that they use function application alone to return a value. Although the Y Combinator can be expressed without using abstraction in the function body, we will opt to define it in a way making use of lambda definitions to present a simpler definition; the definition follows.

Figure 1.29:

$$Y \; = \; \lambda \, f(\lambda \, x \, (f)(x)x) \, \lambda \, x \, (f)(x)x$$

Let's work through an example. Let's say you want to define a function that will evaluate the factorial of a number *n*. Well then the fundamental idea would be to do something like the the function in Figure 1.30.

Figure 1.30:

$$fact \; = \; (lambda \; (n) \; (* \, n \; \ldots))$$

Well the question remains, what should be present instead of the dots? Nothing we have discussed would give any help in answering that, besides the Y Combinator. If you recall from Mathematics, the factorial has an inductive definition like that in Figure 1.31.

Figure 1.31:

$$0! \qquad\qquad\qquad\qquad = 1$$
$$n! \qquad\qquad\qquad = n \, * \, (n\text{-}1)!$$

Our task is to translate this into our Symbolic Language; however, we wish to generalize this idea a bit, not to add a special expression type for every inductive definition we think of. Hence our duty is to make a factorial function which is self-aware, if you will. The function in Figure 1.32 is a rough form of the concept.

Figure 1.32:

$$fact = (lambda\ (fact\ n)\ (*\ n\ (fact\ (pred\ n))))$$

There remains one issue! We have not handled the base case present in our prior definition. To achieve this in the Lambda Calculus we will utilize an if statement; this use case was alluded to earlier.

Figure 1.33:

$$
\begin{aligned}
&fact = (lambda\ (fact\ n) \\
&\quad (if \\
&\qquad (zero?\ n) \\
&\qquad (succ\ 0) \\
&\qquad (*\ n\ (fact\ (pred\ n)))))
\end{aligned}
$$

This is a complete realization of the definition, but there remains one problem. How are we to pass *fact* the value of *fact*? This is when the Y Combinator comes in. The invocation of $(Y fact)$ will form a factorial function, aware of itself for the sake of recursion, accepting the single variable n.

1.5.5 Conclusion

We have now laid a good foundation upon which our Symbolic Expressions can exist. As should be expected, lists will be our primary data-structure in our language of S-Expressions.

1.6   Special Forms of S-Expressions

1.6.1   Numbers

Returning to our prior definition of numbers, we will now define arbitrarily long strings of decimal digits. As you can see, the patterns in Figure 1.34 define numbers by either matching single digits and defining them as a successor, or by matching leading digits and a final digit and evaluating them separately.

Figure 1.34:

$$
\begin{aligned}
1 &= (succ\ 0) \\
2 &= (succ\ 1) \\
&\cdots \\
9 &= (succ\ 8) \\
ten &= (succ\ 9) \\
d\ldots 0 &= (mul\ d\ldots\ ten) \\
d\ldots 1 &= (sum\ (mul\ d\ldots\ ten)\ 1) \\
&\cdots \\
d\ldots 9 &= (sum\ (mul\ d\ldots\ ten)\ 9)
\end{aligned}
$$

Hopefully the rules in Figure 1.34 are a clear embodiment of our decimal number system. Place value is achieved by two measures, (a) inductive definition, and (b) multiplication by ten. This pattern of recursive definition and symbolic pattern matching will be at the heart of our language constructs.

1.6.2   Predicate for Atoms

We will at times need a way of telling whether a given value is a list of an atom; however, because of our decision to use the untyped lambda calculus, we do not have such abilities innately. We will for now take the existence of such a function for granted, as it could be created by simply opting for atoms which wrapped their values in a list describing type, for example. This practice of wrapping values is described as a Monad, and we will discuss these in a later chapter. The reason that we feel comfortable skipping over this defintion is that we will eventually define the language in terms of itself. At that time, the *atom* function would not be necessary, as we could wrap the atoms in a Monadic way. Rather than dwell on this concept, we will define an *atom?* function as a special syntax.

Figure 1.35:

$$(atom? \ (a \ b \dots)) \qquad \Longrightarrow \quad \#f$$
$$(atom? \ a) \qquad\qquad\quad \Longrightarrow \quad \#t$$

1.6.3 List Literals

We define our lists inductively based on the pair-constructing *cons* function we defined earlier. We choose to name this function *quote* because it is treating the entire expression as a literal, rather than as a symbolic expression. More importantly, the syntax of passed lists is indistinguishable from a regular S-Expression, hence we are utilizing the *quoted* form of such an expression.

The definition in Figure 1.36 has a rather sensitive notation. Quotes show that an atomic value, that is, a value referred to in our grammar as $< atom >$ or more importantly, a value referred to as $< var >$ in our grammar of the Lambda Calculus, is being matched. This is unique from most cases in which a portion of a pattern is being labeled by a variable. Additionally, the italicized *ab...* is meant to label the first letter and rest of a string as *a* and *b*, respectively.

In addition to defining the *quote* function, we will provide a shorthand for the operation. So often will we need to define list literals that it makes perfect sense for us to make it as brief as possible.

Quoted forms will come up often in writing list literals, atomic values derived from strings, i.e., *atoms*, and forming more complex data-structures from lists such as tables.

1.6.4 Equality

We have built up an array of atomic values, and a way of keeping them literal. Now we need a way of recognizing them, by means of equivalence. *eq* already solves this problem for numbers, but not

Figure 1.36:

$(quote\ (a))$	$\implies$	$cons\ a\ nil$
$(quote\ (a\ rest \ldots))$	$\implies$	$(cons\ (quote\ a)\ (quote\ (rest \ldots)))$
$(quote\ a\ rest \ldots)$	$\implies$	$(cons\ (quote\ a)\ (quote\ (rest \ldots)))$
$(quote\ "0")$	$\implies$	0
$\ldots$		
$(quote\ "99")$	$\implies$	99
$\ldots$		
$(quote\ "ab \ldots")$	$\implies$	$(cons\ a\ (quote\ b \ldots))$
$(quote\ "a")$	$\implies$	$(cons\ 97\ nil)$
$\ldots$		
$(quote\ "z")$	$\implies$	$(cons\ 122\ nil)$

Figure 1.37:

$$'a \implies (quote\ a)$$

for other quoted atoms. We generalize *eq* to all expressions in our definition of *equal?*.

Figure 1.38:

$(equal?\ (a\ b \ldots)\ (c\ d \ldots))$

$\implies\ (and$

$(equal?\ a\ c)$

$(equal?\ (b \ldots)\ (d \ldots)))$

$(equal?\ a\ b)$ $\implies\ (eq\ a\ b)$

The definition in Figure 1.38 is inductive in nature. It provides a base case in which equivalence is determined by the Lambda Calculus definition of *eq*, and an inductive step in which lists are equivalent only if their constituents are equal.

1.6.5 Variable Definition

Now we add some *syntactic sugar* that will make it easier to store values that will be used in an expression. *let* and *let** set a single value and a list of values, respectively, to be utilized in a given expression. *letrec* takes this idea in another direction, performing the Y-Combinator on a passed function to prepare it for recursion in the passed expression.

Once again we provide an inductive definition, and here we finally utilize the Y Combinator we discussed with regard to recursive functions.

1.6.6 Conclusion

We have formed a basic language consisting of Symbolic Expressions defined by the Lambda Calculus. All of our expressions are reducible to Lambda forms, yet clearer or more concise given their symbolic form. This language will be utilized for expression of all sorts of computational ideas, including algorithms, simulators, and interpreters. Our choice of syntax was purely aesthetic; Lambda Calculus is sufficient for communication with machine, however, our language of Symbolic Expressions is far friendlier to a human reader. This motivation reveals the additional motivation for our

Figure 1.39:

(*let var val expr*)

⟹   ((*lambda* (*var*) *expr*) *val*)

(*let* ∗ ((*var val*)) *expr*)

⟹   (*let var val expr*)

(*let* ∗ ((*var val*) *rest* ...) *expr*)

⟹   ((*lambda* (*var*) (*let* ∗ (*rest* ...) *expr*)) *val*)

(*letrec var fn expr*)

⟹   (*let var* (*Y* (*lambda f fn*)) *expr*)

construction of this language, to form a clear, formal, extensible, and uniform means of communicating ideas.

Chapter 2

Designing Primitive Procedures

2.1   Introduction

We have formed a language constituent of Symbolic Expressions. Additionally, we have an array of useful and primitive Lambda Calculus functions at our disposal. Now in order to build expressive and powerful programs, it will be helpful to define a library of useful Symbolic Functions for manipulation of the various data-types we have formed by abstraction.

2.2   Predicates

We begin with a trivial example, a boolean inverter. Our definition is listed as an S-Expression because when we are ready to make use of it, we will include that pair in a call to *let∗*. The name of the function is the first element, because this is the variable to which it will be assigned. The actual function definition is very familiar. We form a lambda of a single function that results in conditional behavior; if x is true, it results in f, but if x is false, it results in t.

Now we add to our current assortment of numeric predicates the functions $<$ and $>$. These predicates are lambdas accepting two values, that they may be compared. With less-than-equal-to already defined as *leq*, both of these relations are trivial to define.

An important conveniency to note in the forms of Figure 2.2, is their nature given their Lambda Calculus definitions. That is, since

Figure 2.1:

$(not\ (lambda\ (x)\ (if\ x\ \#f\ \#t)))$

Figure 2.2:

$(<\qquad (lambda\ (x\ y)\ (and\ (leq\ x\ y)\ (not\ (eq\ x\ y)))))$
$(>\qquad\qquad\quad (lambda\ (x\ y)\ (not\ (leq\ x\ y))))$

they compile down to a curried form of a function, in other words, a function returning a function, they are very nice to work with. Let's look at an example form and apply appropriate reductions to get a better view of this function's nature.

Figure 2.3:

$(>\ 2)$
$\Longrightarrow\qquad\qquad ((lambda\ (x\ y)\ (not\ (leq\ x\ y)))\ 2)$
$\Longrightarrow\qquad\qquad (lambda\ (y)\ (not\ (leq\ 2\ y)))$

What we see is that when a single value is passed, we achieve a convenient function ready to compare in terms of that parameter. This may seem obvious, familiar, or redundant, but the convenience of this fact should not be taken for granted. This phenomenon is known as currying; it can prove very useful in providing clearness to your expressions; our look at > was only an example of what is going on in all of the functions we discuss.

This ability to supply the arguments of a function one at a time makes for very legible code. Below is an example of an inductive definition utilizing this functionality. The predicate is < with the first argument supplied as two, the step is the *pred* function, and the combinator is multiplication.

This reads very well, as "perform induction while greater than 2 from 6 by means of decrement combining with multiplication",

Figure 2.4:

```
(letrec
   induct
   (lambda
     (induct pred num step combo)
     (if
       (pred num)
       num
       (combo num (induct pred (step num) step combo)))))
   (induct (> 2) 6 pred *))
⟹   720
```

i.e., find the factorial of 6. Let's look at another instance of this, taking advantage of the interchangeability of the definition, and once again of partial function application. This time we induce addition up to and at five, stepping by two in each step up from one.

Figure 2.5:

```
(letrec
   induct
      . . .
      (induct (< 5) 1 (+ 2) +))
⟹   16
```

Our answer coincides with what you would expect, the sum of odd numbers one through seven. Hopefully you feel that our language displays complexity well. The example in Figure 2.5 handled a very generic problem type elegantly and concisely. It is thanks to our adding of abstraction as we go that we are able to make these creations both clear and versatile, and ones in which the creator can take pride.

Lastly we provide predicates to determine whether a given number is even or odd. This function is once again very easy given our convenient Lambda Calculus primitives. The two functions in Figure 2.6 simply check for a specific value of the modulus division by two applied to a number; this is the essence of parity.

Figure 2.6:

(odd?   *(lambda (x) (eq (mod x 2) 1)))*
(even?   *(lambda (x) (eq (mod x 2) 0)))*

Use cases for these two predicates will arise later, but for now they are good at their simple duties, determining parity.

2.3   Higher-Order Functions

In writing clear and concise expressions, it is often useful to have at your disposal higher-order functions (*HOF*), that is, functions that (a) return functions, (b) accept functions as arguments, or (c) do both *a* and *b*.

Hopefully you caught something odd in what I just said, the fact that everything, hence any possible argument or resultant value, is a function! However since we have defined some primitive datatypes, I am referring to non-data-symbolizing functions. This may seem a fine line, but you will often see this terminology tossed around, so you may as well utilize it even in when in the purest of functional languages.

We begin with a couple of type (c) HOFs. The first of the functions in Figure 2.7 serves to flip the argument ordering of a given function, and the second composes two functions.

Figure 2.7:

(flip   *(lambda (func a b) (func b a)))*
(compose   *(lambda (f g) (lambda (arg) (f (g arg)))))*

The function *flip* is very convenient when aiming to apply only the second argument of a function, leaving the other free. The design of *flip* is quite simple, it merely accepts a function, then two arguments, and returns application of them in reverse order. Despite the simplicity of its operation, it can very greatly reduce the complexity of an expression. As an example, look at the definition of a singleton constructori in Figure 2.8, that is, a creator of a pair with a single element.

Figure 2.8:

$((flip\ cons)\ nil)$

compose allows the results of various manipulations to be piped from one to another. A beautiful example of this is a linear function creator. Below is the function accepting slope and y-intercept as its two arguments.

Figure 2.9:

$(lambda\ (m\ b)$
$(compose$
$(+\ b)$
$(*\ m)))$

One of the most important HOFs is defined next. *fold* serves to accumulate a list of values into a single resultant value, based on a function of combination and a starting value. Note that this function is recursive and will be provided using *letrec*. Other functions accepting their name as the first argument should be assumed to follow the same practice.

Our definition of *fold* is as a manipulator of a list returning an accumulated value at the end of a list, and at other points recursing with the *cdr* of the list and an accumulator as determined by the passed function. If the meaning of *fold* is still unclear to you, consider some of these examples.

Figure 2.10:

$(fold\ (lambda\ (fold\ func\ accum\ lst)$
$\quad (if\ (null?\ lst)$
$\qquad accum$
$\qquad (fold\ func\ (func\ accum\ (car\ lst))\ (cdr\ lst)))))$

Figure 2.11:

$(fold\ +\ 0\ '(1\ 2\ 3))\ \implies\ 6$
$(fold\ *\ 0\ '(1\ 2\ 3\ 4))\ \implies\ 24$

As you can now see, the folding of an infix operation $a \bullet b$ over a sequence $a, b, c, \ldots$ is the nested application of the operation, or the effect exhibited by Figure 2.12.

Figure 2.12:

$(\ \ldots\ ((a\ \bullet\ b)\ \bullet\ c)\ \ldots\ )$

As a complement to *fold* we define *reduce*. *reduce* is just like *fold* except right-associative; Hence the function applications are nested just like the *cons* basis of these lists.

Our definition of *reduce* is as a manipulator of a list returning an accumulated value at the end of a list, and at other points returning a manipulation of a recursion with the *cdr*, manipulated by the passed function. If we do an expansion of an infix operator for *reduce* as we did for *fold* we achieve something like the visual in Figure 2.14 when dealing with a list $\ldots, x, y, z$

Together *reduce* and *fold* are sufficient basis for any iterative process. Now we will provide an inverse operation for constructing a list given a construction criterion. *unfold* serves to invert a folding.

Figure 2.13:

$(reduce\ (lambda\ (reduce\ func\ end\ lst)$
$\quad (if\ (null?\ lst)$
$\qquad end$
$\qquad (func\ (car\ lst)\ (reduce\ func\ end\ (cdr\ lst)))))))$

Figure 2.14:

$(\ \ldots\ (x\ \bullet\ (y\ \bullet\ z))\ \ldots\ )$

Figure 2.15:

$(unfold\ (lambda\ (unfold\ func\ init\ pred)$
$\quad (if\ (pred\ init)$
$\qquad (cons\ init\ nil)$
$\qquad (cons\ init\ (unfold\ func\ (func\ init)\ pred)))))$

To clarify the distinction between *fold* and *reduce*, we display the manner in which they can be thought of as opposites.

Figure 2.16:

$$(fold\ (flip\ cons)\ nil\ '(1\ 2\ 3)) \qquad \Longrightarrow \quad '(1\ 2\ 3)$$
$$(reduce\ cons\ nil\ '(1\ 2\ 3)) \qquad \Longrightarrow \quad '(1\ 2\ 3)$$

This examples drives home that the difference between the two is in direction of association, *reduce* is the natural operation for right associative operations and *fold* for left associative operations.

Together our definitions of *fold* and *reduce* are sufficient for definition of any iterative process. *unfold* in addition provides us with a means of constructing arbitrary lists based on constructing rules. We will now implement a variety of derived iterative forms based on *fold* and *reduce*.

2.4   Reductive Forms

We begin with some extensions to our basic binary operators of arithmetic and boolean algebra. The structure of these definitions is similar to that of our early definitions of arithmetic, an iterative process on a base value; however, in this case the conditions and multitude of application are determined by a provided list.

All of the following forms, which we will refer to as *Reductive Forms* are dependent on *fold*. *fold* provides the generic versatile power to combine a list in an arbitrary way; hence you will see a variety of operations used in folding, so you may want to think back to the examples of the nested operator.

We begin with some definitions of arithmetic and boolean manipulations. The definitions of these forms are intuitive, each with an infix operator which fits the role very intuitively.

Now we expand our application field in defining some optimization functions, *min* and *max*. Both of these works by comparing each element with a running extreme value, swapping if a new extreme is found. The definition of *max* follows, a simple folding onto the higher value.

The application of this function to '(1534), for example, would return 5. Our implementation of *min* is nearly identical, simply

Figure 2.17:

$(sum\ (lambda\ (lst)$ $(fold\ +\ 0\ lst))$
$(product\ (lambda\ (lst)$ $(fold\ *\ 1\ lst))$
$(and\ *\ (lambda\ (lst)$ $(fold\ and\ \#t\ lst))$
$(or\ *\ (lambda\ (lst)$ $(fold\ or\ \#f\ lst))$

Figure 2.18:

$(max\ (list)$
   $(fold$
     $(lambda\ (old\ new)$
       $(if\ (>\ old\ new)\ old\ new))$
     $(car\ list)$
     $(cdr\ list)))$

changing the criterion of the fold.

Figure 2.19:

$(min$
$\quad (list)$
$\quad (fold$
$\qquad (lambda\ (old\ new)$
$\qquad\quad (if\ (>\ old\ new)\ old\ new))$
$\qquad (car\ list)$
$\qquad (cdr\ list)))$

Next we define some methods that aid in treatment of lists in their entirety, *length* and *reverse*. *length* is one of the simplest folds you could define, folding by increment. *reverse* on the other hand, is not as obvious in its means of operation; it folds by means of a swap operation, (*flipcons*), in this way forming a fully reversed list.

Figure 2.20:

$(length \quad (lambda\ (lst)\ (fold\ (lambda\ (x\ y)\ (+\ x\ 1))\ 0\ lst)))$
$(reverse \qquad\quad (lambda\ (lst)\ (fold\ (flip\ cons)\ nil\ lst)))$

Now we provide a special function for determining associations in a list meant as a table. The setup of these lists is like the structure in Figure 2.21, where each element is a list, with the first element serving as a key, and the second serving as a value.

In determining the association, we *fold* with the aim of reaching a value with a key matching that for which we are searching.

assoc is very important in modeling hash-tables, and in general keeping track of named values. If *assoc* were applied to the table displayed prior with *banana* as a key, it would evaluate to *yellow*. Here is the full form, with *table* referring to the aforementioned table.

Figure 2.21:

```
'((apple              red)
  (pear             green)
  (banana          yellow))
```

Figure 2.22:

```
(assoc (lambda (x list)
  (fold
    (lambda (accum item)
      (if
        (equal? item (car x))
        (cdr x)
        accum)))
    #f
    list)))
```

Figure 2.23:

$$(assoc\ 'banana\ table) \implies 'yellow$$

2.5   List Manipulations

Before we delve too far into manipulation of lists, we will define a
very helpful list constructor as follows.

Figure 2.24:

(list
    (lambda (list a)
        (if (null? a)
            nil
            (lambda (rest)
                (cons a (list rest)))))

Usage of *list* is very intuitive. To construct a list, pass each element as argument to the *list* function, ending with *nil*. Figure 2.25
has an example of usage.

Figure 2.25:

(list 1 2 3 *nil)* $\implies$ $'$(1 2 3)

In manipulating a list, there are two basic classes of operations,
(a) mapping a list to a value, and (b) converting one list to another.
We have thoroughly covered the former, starting first with general
forms and then implementing some useful examples. Now we will
move on to the latter.

In mapping one list to another, we will provide two generic
functions. The first, *map*, will apply a single function to each element of a list; the second will filter out items based on a predicate.
These functions are very useful, imagine for example finding a sum
of squares or constructing a list of primes.

Our map implementation works as a reduction with *cons*; if this
were the extent of the function, the initial list would be returned.
However, each element is passed through the provided function to
result in a list with modified elements. *filter* takes advantage of

Figure 2.26:

```
(map
  (lambda (func lst)
    (reduce
      (lambda (x y)
        (cons (func x) y))
      nil
      lst)))
```

the same aspect of *reduce*; however, in its definition it casts away values not matching a predicate.

Figure 2.27:

```
(filter
  (lambda (pred lst)
    (reduce
      (lambda (x y)
        (if (pred x) (cons x y) y))
      nil
      lst)))
```

Let's look at some examples of *map* and *filter*; the extent of their usefulness was alluded to earlier, but in Figure 2.28 are some examples to clarify their usage.

The uses of Figure 2.28 were very clear in their meaning, as one would hope. Now that we have some strong ways of manipulating a list, we will move on to means of adding elements to a list. We provide some functions for appending to a list, either a single element of a list of elements, i.e., *concatenation*. These functions serve as nice complements to the two which were defined earlier, as they allow for expansion to supersets, and the earlier two allow only for constructing a subset.

Figure 2.28:

(map	*(∗ 2) '(1 2 3))*	⟹	*'(2 4 6)*
(filter	*odd? '(1 2 3 4 5 6))*	⟹	*'(1 3 5)*

Figure 2.29:

(push	*(lambda (a b) (reverse (cons b (reverse a)))))*
(concat	*(lambda (a b) (fold push a b)))*

These list manipulations will prove very useful, and given our prior functions, were very concise and clear in definition. Below are some examples of *push* and *concat* applications.

Figure 2.30:

(push	*4 '(1 2 3))*	⟹	*'(1 2 3 4)*
(concat	*'(1 2) '(2 4))*	⟹	*'(1 2 3 4)*

2.6   Conclusion

We have amassed a variety of useful and versatile functions of symbolic expressions. With these in hand, we are ready to build complex and useful programs.

Chapter 3

Simulating Logical Devices

The key innovation in the study of computation was the development of machines for the mechanization of algorithms. Of course, you are familiar with the idea of devices executing algorithms; however, the relationship of our exploration of the Lambda Calculus to such devices may not be immediately evident. In this chapter we will compose with our symbolic language a simulation of different logical devices.

3.1   Turing Machines

Having built up our language to a point of high-level abstraction, we will now try to simulate a trivial computational platform, a Turing Machine. In doing so we will address many key issues like immutability, hash-tables, and, once again, recursion. Additionally, we will become comfortable with the idea of interpreting one platform within another; this ability to interpret is the key to abstraction in computation.

3.1.1   A Ruleset

A Turing Machine computes values based on an initial state, initial values, and rules of transition from a given state and value to a new state and value. The machine itself has a tape full of values and a head which navigates the tape, moving either right of left one slot at any given time. Additionally, this head maintains an idea of state, the mode in which it is observing a given value.

Together these primitive capabilities are enough to compute any algorithm. The usual manipulation could be broken down into a series of steps, most likely represented as different states. Each state, in turn, maintains a specific array of ways in which to manipulate read values, and in which direction to move in each case.

All of this methodology is governed by a single ruleset. Hence to simulate one, we will undoubtedly need a representation of these rules. The structure in Figure 3.1 is one way, and the way which we will choose, of representing such a set. We have already seen use of lists as hash-tables, so this should not be a surprising design decision.

Figure 3.1:

$$(let$$
$$rules$$
$$'(((A\ 0)\ (1\ R\ H))$$
$$((A\ 1)\ (0\ R\ H)))$$
$$\dots)$$

A ruleset like the one in Figure 3.1 serves to tell a simulation in what way to behave given a certain input state. Hence together with our earlier defined *assoc* function and an actual executor of the matching behavior, this ruleset will handle all state logic.

3.1.2   Fundamental States

In order for our simulation to ever end we will need to designate a specific state the *halt-state*. In our implementation, H will signal the end of an algorithm. Additionally, the state in which our machine is initialized will not be the choice of the ruleset, and so we choose to once again arbitrarily designate a specific state value for this case. The state named A will be the initialization state of all simulations.

Given these determined special states, we will need to set the initial state and provide checking for the halt state. Hence our recursive, rule-applying function needs to accept a state, as well as head position, rules, state, and tape values, and to check whether it is in the halt state. If this is not the case, it will then apply the current rule and repeat.

3.1.3 Mutability

The Lambda Calculus does not allow for mutation of values, thus we will need to model this behavior by maintaining a modified value upon each change, one that is the response of a given function. Let's work out an example of working around immutability in lists.

Figure 3.2:

```
(set
  (lambda
    (key val hash)
    (map
    (lambda
      (item)
      (if
        (equal? (car item) key)
        (cons key (cons val))
        item))
    hash)))
```

In this case we utilized *map* to cycle through the items of the hash. Within the map we substituted for the value with the specified key. In our writing to the tape, we will need to use similar tactics.

A Turing Machine writes a value to a specific slot of its tape, namely, the slot upon which the head is currently resting. Within our simulator, this slot is specified by the current index of the simulation. Hence, the writing function we will require is one designed to write to a specific index of a tape.

In the function definition of Figure 3.3, we recurse with the tail of the list until we reach the specified index, and we then perform the substitution, ending recursion.

Figure 3.3:

```
(letrec write-rule
  (lambda (write-rule tape index rule)
  (if
    (null? tape)
    tape
    (if
      (equal? index 0)
      (cons (car rule) (cdr tape))
      (cons (car tape) (write-rule (cdr tape) (− index 1) rule)))))
```

Above, we defined write-rule as a recursive function accepting a tape, index, and rule. If we have run out of tape, we return the empty tape; however, if we have tape left we take one of two paths in evaluation. If the index to which we wish to write is zero, we return the rule-specified value embedded into the list where the first item previously would have resided. If, however, we are writing to another index, we simply reduce the problem to writing to the item one less in index on tape, excluding the first item.

3.1.4   The Event Loop

The simulation is based on the idea of following rule to rule until the algorithm terminates. Hence rules are executed recursively until the halt-state is reached. At this point, a final table is returned. The iteration function is defined in Figure 3.4.

This *iterate* function definition utilized *letrec* to receive itself as an argument. Its use of this value is subtly different from our past use cases. In *iterate*, we pass the function itself as an argument to another function, iterate-rule. For this reason, we can call *iterate* and iterate-rule *mutually recursive*, that is, because *iterate* invokes iterate-rule and iterate-rule in turn invokes *iterate*.

There are multiple dependencies to the function definition which we have not yet defined. In the following section we will put them all together with the *iterate* function and achieve our final goal of simulation.

Figure 3.4:

```
(letrec iterate (lambda
    (iterate index rules state tape)
    (if
        (equal? state 'H)
        tape
        (iterate-rule
            iterate
            (cadr (assoc (list state index) rules))
            rules
            index
            tape)))
```

3.1.5   A Simulator

All of the above principles can be combined to form a Turing Machine simulator. The definition of *iterate* is dependent upon a few
helper functions. First of all, there are a couple very basic shorthands which are defined in Figure 3.5.

Figure 3.5:

```
(cadr              (lambda (x) (car (cdr x))))
(caddr             (lambda (x) (car (cdr (cdr x)))))
```

Now we move on to the functions provided for applying a rule
and for applying a shift in the head. To shift the index we simply
handle the case of right motion, i.e., $'R$ direction as an upward
shift, as well as any other cases.

The definition of *move* in Figure 3.6 is very simple in nature.
A current index and direction of motion are received as argument,
and a new index is then returned. If the direction is $'R$ then the
index will increase, but if it is not, i.e., if it is $'L$, it will decrease.

Figure 3.6:

(move (lambda
   (index motion)
   (if
      (equal? motion 'R)
      (+ 1 index)
      (− 1 index))))

Furthermore, keeping in mind the earlier definition of subtraction based on Lambda Calculus primitives, you will recall that subtracting one from zero will result in zero. This behavior is convenient in this case, avoid strange edge-case behavior.

Example usage of the *move* function would be as follows.

Figure 3.7:

(move 5 'R)	$\implies$	6
(move 3 'L)	$\implies$	2

Now we move on to a prior utilized function for the application of a rule to the tape. The rule applier receives the earlier defined *iterate* function as an argument, and then applies it to the moved index, the ruleset, the rule-provided state, and the new tape.

This function consists only of basic manipulations of the rule to parse out the modifications needing to be applied. With all of the dependencies defined, we achieve the comprehensive definition of a Turing Machine simulator shown in Figure 3.9.

3.1.6   Computation with Turing Machines

A half-adder as a Turing Ruleset would look like the Figure 3.10.

Figure 3.8:

```
(iterate-rule (lambda
    (iterate rule rules index tape)
    (iterate
        (move index (cadr rule))
        rules
        (caddr rule)
        (write-rule tape index rule)))))
```

Figure 3.9:

```
(let*
    ((index 0)
     (rules '(((A 0) (1 R H))))
     (state 'A)
     (cadr (...))
     (caddr (...))
     (move (lambda
         (index motion)
         (...))
     (iterate-rule (lambda
         (iterate rule rules index tape)
         (...))
     (letrec write-rule (lambda
         (write-rule tape index rule)
         (...))
         (letrec iterate (lambda
         (iterate index rules state tape)
         (...))
     (write (iterate index rules state '(0 0 0)))))))
```

Figure 3.10:

(let

  rules

  '(((A 0) (0 R Z))

    ((A 1) (1 R C))

    ((Z 0) (0 R H))

    ((Z 1) (1 L N))

    ((C 0) (1 L N))

    ((C 1) (0 L Y))

    ((N 0) (0 R H))

    ((N 1) (0 R H))

    ((Y 0) (1 R H))

    ((Y 1) (1 R H)))

  (write (iterate 0 rules 'A '(0 0 0)))))

3.2   Circuits

Circuits are quite different in nature from the previously discussed Turing Machine. The main reason for this difference is that components, analogous to the prior discussed rules, are dependent directly upon each other, while in a Turing Machine a single processing unit handled transitions between states.

3.2.1   Structure of Circuits

Our model of circuits will consist of two component types, (a) relational boxes, and (b) wires. Relational boxes are atomic relations between circuit values, accepting input as electrical signals and outputting an electrical signal. Wires serve to connect these boxes to each other, bearing these electrical signals in one of two sates. A wire bearing current is said to have the boolean value true (t), but a wire without current is said to be of the boolean value false (f).

Now, given these ideas of relational boxes and wires, we add abstraction to reach a view of relational boxes as logical primitives. For example, there may be a relational box named *gateA* which accepts a single wire and maps to the specified outputs in Figure 3.11.

Figure 3.11:

$(gateA \#t)$ $\implies$ $\#f$
$(gateA \#f)$ $\implies$ $\#t$

Of course, this sort of truth table maintains an electrical interpretation. Specifically, such a relational box would output current when receiving no current, but would output no current if receiving current.

The relational boxes we will take as primitive are similar to our boolean operators already defined. We utilize an and-gate, an or-gate, and a not-gate. The first two gates accept two wires as input values and output to another wire a current value based on their logical operation. Hence an and-gate accepting two current-bearing wires will direct current to its output wire. A not-gate on the other hand accepts a single wire for input value and outputs the opposite value to another wire.

To begin our design of circuits, we design a relation constituent of the boolean operators listed above as primitives.

Figure 3.12:

```
(half-adder
    (lambda (a b)
    (let*
        ((s (and (or a b) (not (and a b))))
         (r (and a b)))
        (cons r (cons s nil)))))
```

The procedure in Figure 3.12 is known as a half-adder. Given two bits as input, this procedure determines the added value, including any carried value. Recall that our language was designed not only for evaluation by machine, but for representation of ideas like the one presented above.

The methodology of the half-adder should be for the most part apparent. Given input values named a and b, output values named s and r need to be determined. s is true when one, but not both, of the inputs is true, and r when both are true. Hence s represents the first digit of a binary result, and r the second or carried value.

Let's look at some examples of the behavior of a half-adder.

Figure 3.13:

(half-adder #f #f)	$\implies$	$'$(#f #f)
(half-adder #f #t)	$\implies$	$'$(#f #t)
(half-adder #t #f)	$\implies$	$'$(#f #t)
(half-adder #t #t)	$\implies$	$'$(#t #f)

If you are not familiar with the behavior of binary digits when adding, note that the examples in Figure 3.13 exhibit the basics of this behavior. If we were to represent current instead by either 1 or 0, we would achieve the more clearly binary behavior shown in Figure 3.14.

Figure 3.14:

(half-adder 0 0)	$\implies$	$'$(0 0)
(half-adder 0 1)	$\implies$	$'$(0 1)
(half-adder 1 0)	$\implies$	$'$(0 1)
(half-adder 1 1)	$\implies$	$'$(1 0)

Hopefully this example has helped to illustrate the emergence of relatively high- level ideas like arithmetic from basic controlled flow of current. In the following sections we will attempt to depart from a purely boolean-arithmetic driven outlook on circuits toward a generic circuit structure definition process and simulator.

3.2.2 Inter-Dependency

In our presentation of circuit design, we utilized *let** to display relations in order of their dependency. However, you will notice that we repeated some computations without separating them out, and more importantly that all computed values were statically set to a primitive manipulation, never to be changed. Hence, our prior definition does not accurately model an actual circuit; currents cannot be updated and changes cannot propagate.

To better reflect the reality of circuit design, we will allow a circuit structure to be defined *holistically* and *symbolically*, and for this structure to be utilized to compute the values of individual components. To say that our structure will be defined holistically means that the entire circuit blueprint may be laid prior to any computation, which brings us to our next point. Since definition will be symbolic, using names rather than values, our relations can be established between yet-to-be-defined values.

We will use a table like those which we have already seen for our basic data- structure. The table will be built up with named components, each being manipulations of the circuit. We begin with a basic realization of this idea.

Figure 3.15:

```
(get-gate
  (lambda
    (name env)
    (assoc name env)))
(set-gate
  (lambda
    (name value env)
    (set name value env)))
```

The definitions in Figure 3.15 are simply aliases to the *assoc* and *set* functions of regular hash-tables. We have yet to implement the idea of gates as manipulations of the circuit. In order to do this, we will need a clear means of applying a manipulation to a given object. This idea is key to an object-oriented outlook on programming which we will discuss in the following.

3.2.3   Methods on Objects

There is a paradigm in programming known as object oriented
programming. Under this methodology, everything is an object
containing data and behavior, *values* and *methods*. We have already seen the functional architecture for associated values, that
is, a table or list of pairs. However, the key to this object- oriented
approach is that the methods are not regular functions but, rather,
maintain a context in which they operate. These methods of an
object should operate upon the object itself. To simulate this idea
in our language, we will make all methods a function of the object
in which they exist. Hence we can define a generic method applier
as follows.

Figure 3.16:

> (*method*
>   (*lambda*
>   (*obj mname*)
>   ((*assoc mname obj*) *obj*)))

Usage of this convenience function would then look like the
Figure 3.17, applying a named function to an object.

Figure 3.17:

> (*method person 'greet*)

In this case *person* serves as an object, and *greet* as a named
method on that object. What does it mean to be an object? In the
case of our implementation, an object is merely a data-structure,
like any other table; however, the distinctive trait is the inclusion of
methods. Methods allow for the coupling of functions to a specific
data-set. In our example in Figure 3.17, a greet function is attached

to the *person*, and easily called by name to perform some action in the specific context of the *person* object.

We will utilize the concepts of object-oriented programming (OOP) in our design of gates. A gate will be a table containing some values and some methods. The only value will be named *value*, the boolean value of the gate, and the methods will be named *get* and *set*, performing the manipulations of the value which their names would suggest. Hence, we would have a basic constructor of a gate like the one in Figure 3.18.

Figure 3.18:

```
(make-gate
    (lambda (value get set)
       (list
           (list 'value value nil)
           (list 'get get nil)
           (list 'set set nil)
           nil)))
```

Given this structure, we redefine our gate getter and setter to simplify interfacing with this structure as follows.

Notice that the main change was in making the get-gate function get the boolean value of a gate rather than the gate itself. set-gate remained a function returning the mutated environment, for the sake of setting up a circuit initially.

3.2.4   Child Object Definitions

A *child* of an object is one inheriting the structure of its parent and either restricting or expanding the construction, value or method interfaces. The function in Figure 3.20 is a child of the gate definition for constant-value gates.

As you were made to expect in our discussion of object-oriented programming, both of the methods accept as their first parameter the gate object itself. The getter and setter are very simple, based around the value attached to the gate object. Building upon this simple architecture, we will define a generic relational gate object.

Figure 3.19:

```
(get-gate
  (lambda
    (name env)
    (let
    gate (assoc name env)
    ((assoc 'get gate) gate env))))
(set-gate
  (lambda
    (name value env)
    (set name value env)))
```

Figure 3.20:

```
(const-gate
  (lambda
    (value)
    (make-gate
    value
    (lambda (obj env) (assoc 'value obj))
    (lambda (obj value) (set 'value value obj)))))
```

Figure 3.21:

```
(fn-gate
  (lambda
    (fn a b)
    (make-gate
      (lambda (a b) (fn a b))
      (lambda (obj env)
        ((assoc 'value obj)
         (get-gate a env)
         (get-gate b env))
        (lambda (obj value) obj)))))
```

The definition in Figure 3.21 makes the value of the gate a method as well. The getter then applies the *value* method to the *get*-wrapped values of the two input components. The relation tying together these input components is passed as the first argument to the fn-gate constructor. This is to say that when getting the value of an fn-gate, the values upon which it depends will be gotten as well in a sort of cascading dependency. These dependencies will then be assessed based on the function specific to that instance of fn-gate, maybe logical or, for example.

We now define, in turn, children of the fn-gate constructor easily as follows.

Figure 3.22:

```
(or-gate        (fn-gate (lambda (a b) (or a b))))
(and-gate       (fn-gate (lambda (a b) (or a b))))
(not-gate       (fn-gate (lambda (a b) (not b)) #f))
```

3.2.5   A Simulator

Putting together all prior defined functions we have the simulator
in Figure 3.23.

Figure 3.23:

```
(let*
  ((pairing
     (lambda (a b) (...)))
   (make-gate
     (lambda (value get set) (...)))
   (const-gate
     (lambda (value) (...)))
   (get-gate
     (lambda (name env) (...)))
   (set-gate
     (lambda (name value env) (...)))
   (fn-gate
     (lambda (fn a b) (...)))
   (or-gate (fn-gate (lambda (a b) (...))))
   (and-gate (fn-gate (lambda (a b) (...))))
   (not-gate (fn-gate (lambda (a b) (...)) #f)))
  (...))
```

3.2.6   Computation with Circuits

A half-adder utilizing our simulator would look like Figure 3.24.

Figure 3.24:

(let∗
    ((*env* (set-gate *'a* (const-gate #*t*) *env*))
    (*env* (set-gate *'b* (const-gate #*t*) *env*))
    (*env* (set-gate *'*1 (or-gate *'a 'b*) *env*))
    (*env* (set-gate *'*2 (and-gate *'a 'b*) *env*))
    (*env* (set-gate *'*3 (not-gate *'*2) *env*))
    (*env* (set-gate *'*4 (and-gate *'*1 *'*3) *env*)))
    (*cons* (get-gate *'*4 *env*) (*cons* (get-gate *'*2 *env*) *nil*)))

Chapter 4

Mechanical Interpretation of a Language

The most important revelation in learning the art of programming is that the language in which you work is completely arbitrary. More specifically, the language in which you express concepts was defined in terms of another language at some point. We have already made clear this concept in our definition of our symbolic language. We now turn to the interpretation of one language within another.

4.1   Lambda Calculus

The language which we will interpret is one with which we are already familiar, Lambda Calculus. The Lambda Calculus has very simple syntax and will thus not be too hard to interpret. Recall the syntax, which is composed of the following expressions.

- A variable reference.

- A function definition of the form λab where a is a variable reference and b is an expression.

- A function application of the form $(a)b$ where a is an expression, as is b.

Note that the generality of the third form, function application, is what gives this syntax its description as the Untyped Lambda Calculus. Since no qualification is given to the expression which will be passed argument, this language is without types.

4.1.1   Lambda Calculus in S-Expressions

In expression the Lambda Calculus in S-Expressions, we will utilize the *quote* function as well as the structure inherent of parenthetical expressions in these expressions. Hence an example of an expression which could be evaluated is the one presented in Figure 4.1.

Figure 4.1:

$'(lam\ x\ lam\ y\ (x)\ y)$

4.1.2   An Evaluator

We define our evaluator pretty easily. Note that we will begin by defining an *apply* function. This function accepts a function and list of arguments, and then applies each of these arguments to a lambda one by one.

Figure 4.2:

$(define$ (apply-set $fn\ args)$
$\quad (if$
$\quad\quad (null?\ args)$
$\quad\quad fn$
$\quad\quad$ (apply-set $(fn\ (car\ args))\ (cdr\ args))))$

Just like our definition of the syntax, our evaluator handles variable reference, lambda definition, and function application.

Variable reference is a problem very easily solved. Atoms are considered variable references, and hence serve as keys in accessing values from the environment hash.

Function definition is achieved by returning a lambda of a single variable for expressions of the necessary form. Within the lambda, the passed argument is appended to the environment with the argument name as its key. The function body is then evaluated.

Function application is the default case, thus we match against the antecedent t. The applier apply-set is then called with the evaluated form of the first argument and the evaluated arguments. This architecture is an explicit choice *not* to opt for a lazy method of evaluation.

Figure 4.3:

```
(evallam (lambda (evallam expr env)
    (cond (((atom? expr) (assoc expr env))
          ((equal? (car expr) 'lam)
            (lambda (x)
              (evallam
                (cddr expr)
                (set (cadr expr) x env))))
          ((null? (cdr expr))
            (evallam (car expr) env))
          (#t
            (apply-set
              (evallam (car expr) env)
              (map
                (lambda (expr) (evallam expr env))
                (cdr expr)))))))))
```

4.1.3 Evaluation of Forms

An example of a form which could be evaluated is presented in Figure 4.4.

Figure 4.4:

$'(lam\ x\ lam\ y\ ((x)\ y)\ 1)$

4.2   Flat-Input Lambda Calculus

In the prior implementation of an interpreter, we took advantage of the structure inherent to a nested S-Expression. This approach was sufficient for our initial purposes; however, to separate our interpreter from the details of its use within our Symbolic Language, we will now allow its interpretation to apply to a flat list of atoms. In order to represent the expression previously expressed by nested S-Expressions, we will now utilize some symbols which will represent parenthetical expressions. The expression in Figure 4.5 is an example of this new flat structure.

Figure 4.5:

$'(lam\ x\ lam\ y\ <\ x\ >\ y)$

Of course, this use of $<>$ symbols would extend to any instance of parentheses in our prior method.

With our new, less inherently structured approach, we will need to provide an additional layer of parsing. Parsing will provide this missing aspect of structure. Parsing parentheses is actually our most complex algorithm yet attempted. We will take this algorithm's implementation as an opportunity to experiment with the second style of programming we have yet to investigate, imperative programming.

4.2.1   The Two Styles of Programming

There are two basic approaches to programming, derived from the two original theories of computation. We have talked far more about functional programming tactics in prior sections of this book, leaving imperative programming on the sidelines. However, the problem at hand is a great case study in the relation between imperative and functional languages. We will begin with an imperative implementation, and then port the code over to our current language of choice.

4.2.2 Imperative Constructs

In our exploration of imperative programming, we will encounter a few new operators, and utilize some new idioms. We will provide a purely functional, that is, without mutation, implementation of these constructs as well. In later chapters, we will be able to automate the utilization of these analogs identified.

4.2.3 Mutators

The main difference between imperative and *purely* functional programming is the presence of mutability. In functional programs, a value can be defined but not mutated; however, when taking the imperative approach, values will often be set to a new value after their definition. The code in Figure 4.6 is an example of this behavior.

Figure 4.6:

$$(define\ x\ 5)$$
$$(set!\ x\ (*\ 2\ x))$$
$$\implies\ x\ =\ 10$$

The *define* operator serves to allocate a variable and initiate it with a value. This variable, x, can then be accessed throughout the procedure, and even mutated to equal a new value. In the example, it was initiated as 5, but *set!* to 10.

In order to simulate mutation, we will need a means of manipulating an environment accessed and mutated by a myriad of expressions. The pure means of achieving this, as we have previously discussed, is to call a function with a mutated duplicate of the environment. In this case, that function would be defined to use recursion.

Our recursive function will accept an environment and an expression address, i.e., index, as argument, and return either the

result or a recursion with a mutated environment and at a different expression address. This contraption is similar to a register
machine in many ways; an analog which we will further analyze
in later sections. What follows is an implementation using these
concepts of the prior imperative procedure.

Figure 4.7:

```
(letrec
  main
  (lambda (main env start)
    (get (list (main (set 'x 5 env) (+ 1 start))
               (main (set 'x (* 2 (assoc 'x env)) env) (+ 1 start))
               (equal? (assoc 'x env) 5)) start))
  ...)
```

In Figure 4.7, note that we omitted the second *equal?*, because
only one of them bore an actual effect. We now move on to address
more complex issues of this impure approach.

In programming languages, *scope* refers to the region over which
a variable is accessible. The scoping of a variable is specified by the
define operator; hence the code in Figure 4.8 is another example of
this behavior.

Figure 4.8:

```
(define x 5)
((lambda (y)
   (set! x y)) 12)
(equal? x 12)
;; #t
```

Of note is the fact that the *define* occurred separate from any
function. This means that the defined variable will now take on
the *global* scope, being accessible and mutable from within any

function.

In translating the definition and application of the lambda to a purely functional procedure, we will provide the action of the lambda as a prelude to the rest of the procedure. The invocation of the lambda will require that we set the index to which the flow of control should return after completion of the lambda. This takes the form of a variable *ret* defined on the environment. All other methods in Figure 4.9 are similar to those in prior procedures.

Figure 4.9:

(letrec
   main
  (lambda (main env start)
   (get (list (main (set 'x (assoc 'y env) env) (assoc 'ret env))
              (main (set 'x 5 env) (+ 1 start))
              (main (set 'ret 3 (set 'y 12 env)) 0)
              (equal? (assoc 'x env) 5)) start))
  ...)

In the Figure 4.9, our starting index would instead be 1, in order to begin at the first line of the imperative program and avoid the definition of the lambda used later on in the procedure.

If the *define* of the prior example had instead occurred within a function definition, as in Figure 4.10, it would only be accessible from within that function, or other functions defined within it.

Figure 4.10:

  (define scope (lambda (x)
    (define y x)))
  (scope 5)
  y
  ;; The written variable, y, will be inaccessible.

In Figure 4.10 we demonstrate definition with a single-function scope. Thus the *define* is fulfilling the same role as *let* did in prior programs. However, since *define* does not accept an expression which it will govern, the example definition is of no effect. In the following section we display a means of making use of this sort of *define* statement.

To simulate this, we would need to add a sort of inner scope to our function calls, exhibited in the form of jumping to another instruction. We will, for the sake of simplicity, create an inner environment, known as a *closure*, as a value on the outer, or normal, environment. Then, prior to returning, we will clear the inner environment by setting it to *nil*.

Of note is the fact that the *define* from within a closure translated into a *set* upon the inner environment. If we were aiming to automate this process, we would instead maintain an image of the original environment, and simply revert to that image after execution of the function.

4.2.4   Multiple Expression Procedures

In our earlier, purely-functional programs, a procedure consisting of multiple expressions would have been no use. Without side-effects, only the final expression could bear any form of result. However, now investigating an imperative approach, a procedure may utilize multiple expressions, each contributing its own mutation to a final effect. Figure 4.12 is an example of this in practice; the syntax is simply a chain of expressions where an individual would have previously existed.

Obviously, this example is of no utility. The desired function could be just as easily achieved with a single expression. Useful examples, however, will present themselves in the following sections.

4.2.5   Loop Constructs

You will often see imperative programming avoiding use of recursion. Rather, these programs will often iterate, mutating the environment in each step. For convenience in utilization of this approach, we define a function for constructing a range over which to iterate.

The definition in Figure 4.13 is pretty straight-forward, much like earlier function definitions. Note that the ranges are of the

Figure 4.11:

```
(letrec
  main
  (lambda (main env start)
    (get
      (list
        (let * ((outer env)
                (inner
                  (set 'y
                    (assoc 'x (assoc 'inner outer))
                    (assoc 'inner outer))
                  (outer (set 'inner inner outer)))
                (main outer (+ 1 start)))
          (main (set 'inner nil outer) (assoc 'ret outer))
          (main
            (set
              'inner
              (set 'x 5 (assoc 'inner env))
              env)
            (+ 1 start))
          (main
        (set 'ret 4 (set 'y 12 env))
            0)
        (assoc 'y env))
      start))
  ...)
```

Figure 4.12:

$(define\ incr\ (lambda\ (x)$
$\quad (define\ y\ (+\ x\ 1))$
$\quad y))$

Figure 4.13:

$(define\ range\ (lambda\ (x)$
$\quad (if\ (equal?\ x\ 0)$
$\quad\quad nil$
$\quad\quad (cons\ (-\ x\ 1)\ (range\ (-\ x\ 1))))))$

form 0, 1, ..., n-1. Here's an example of this function being used to calculate a factorial.

Figure 4.14:

$(define\ fact\ (lambda\ (x)$
$\quad (define\ ans\ 1)$
$\quad (map\ (range\ x)\ (lambda\ (n)$
$\quad\quad (set!\ ans\ (*\ and\ (+\ 1\ n)))))$
$\quad ans))$

The starting value of the answer is 1, just like the sort of inductive definitions we provided earlier in the book. The final answer is then achieved by repeated multiplication performed on the previous *ans*. In the case of 5, for example, the accumulator *ans* takes on the values presented in Figure 4.15.

Figure 4.15:

$$1$$
$$\implies \quad 1 * 1 \quad \implies \quad 1$$
$$\implies \quad 1 * 2 \quad \implies \quad 2$$
$$\implies \quad 2 * 3 \quad \implies \quad 6$$
$$\implies \quad 4 * 6 \quad \implies \quad 24$$
$$\implies \quad 5 * 24 \quad \implies \quad 120$$

4.2.6 An Imperative Solution

Now we will jump right in to the non-trivial problem at hand, restated below.

"Given a string of nested angle-bracket delimited groups, return a nested list containing the contents of these groups. For example, given the list of characters $'(a < bc > d)$ return $'(a(bc)d)$."

Since we are taking an imperative approach, think, "What is the easily defined iterative process underlying this problem?" The answer is clearly navigation of the string, and so we begin with a *range*-based loop that will cycle through each character of the string in order.

Figure 4.16:

```
(define parse (lambda (expr)
   (map (range (length expr)) (lambda (i)
      (define read (get expr i))
      // ...
)))
```

Now we will need to describe a slightly more specific strategy in performing the desired process.

- A parenthetical will be split from the string, with a segment, although possibly an empty one, before and after it.

- Once a parenthetical has been removed, we will need to recurse on these segments, i.e., the parenthetical and the portion after it.

To make our way toward this implementation, we will define a variable *before* that will hold the segment of the string occurring prior to any parenthetical; a variable *accum* that will hold characters that have been read in but whose destination has yet to be determined, in this way serving as a cache; *paren* which will hold a separated out parenthetical; and *found* which will be true if and only if a parenthetical has been parsed.

Figure 4.17:

```
(define parse (lambda (expr)
   (define before)
   (define accum nil)
   (define paren)
   (define found #f)
   (map (range (length expr)) (lambda (i)
     (define read (get expr i))
     // ...
)))
```

In order to parse out the parenthetical, however, we will need an additional variable. This variable will aid us in parsing nested parentheses to separate out the top-level parenthetical.

We will need to handle three obvious classes of characters in our parsing of the parentheses:

- An opening parenthesis.

- A closing parenthesis.

- Any other character.

Additionally, the class of a character may be disregarded if we have already parsed a top-level parenthetical. Its parsing will be handled when we are ready to recurse. siven these additions of case-handling, we insert *if ... else* statements as in Figure 4.18.

Figure 4.18:

```
(define parse (lambda (expr)
  (define before)
  (define accum nil)
  (define paren)
  (define found #f)
  (define nested 0)
  (map (range (length expr)) (lambda (i)
    (define read (get expr i))
    (if (and (equal? ' < read) (not found))
      (..."1. an opening parenthesis" ...)
      (if (and (equal? ' > read) (not found))
        (..."2. a closing parenthesis" ...)
        (..."3. any other character" ...))))))
```

Of course, we will need to combine any separated out parenthetical with the components occurring before and after it to form
the designated response. Hence we provide the following *return*
statement in Figure 4.19.

Now we implement our nesting logic and the final algorithm.
Nesting will be handled based on one of the following occurrences.

- A once nested expression was just opened.

- An expression was just closed to be un-nested.

Parentheses occurred within a nested expression.

The first and second cases are handled under the conditionals for their respective character classes, and in either class under
another nesting case, the third will be handled.

The last components missing from our implementation are the
building up of an accumulator and the setting of the various components to the accumulator. We will implement these portions in
the code of Figure 4.20.

- When the parenthetical is closed, it is recursively *parsed* and
  set to the *paren* variable.

Figure 4.19:

```
(define parse (lambda (expr)
  ..."variables" ...
  (map (range (length expr)) (lambda (i)
    (..."parse" ...))
  (if paren
    (concat (push before paren) (parse accum))
    expr)))
```

- When a parenthetical is open, *before* receives the accumulator value.

4.2.7   From Imperative to Functional

From the final implementation of our program in the previous section we can derive a functional version. The differences will be based on the following principles of functional programming:

- Values shall not be mutated.

- Control-flow shall not be explicit.

- Recursion is a fundamental idea.

Let's begin by abiding to the second rule, inspired by the third. The first thing you will notice is that all variables were made function arguments. This is because in a pure function, the only state is provided by the arguments. Hence when recursing, we will need to pass all required data to the function as argument.

Also of note is the fact that rather than maintain an index of the list on which we are operating, we pass as argument to the recursive call only subsequent characters, i.e., those which have yet to be read. This is both logical in that our progress in navigating the list is maintained, and idiomatic as you have seen in prior programs written in our Symbolic Language.

The final portion of our program includes a definition of *funparse_*. This was merely for convenience, as *funparse_* provides all of the initialization values as argument to *funparse*.

Figure 4.20:

```
(define parse (lambda (expr)
  (define before)
  (define accum nil)
  (define paren)
  (define found #f)
  (define nested 0)
  (map (range (length expr)) (lambda (i)
    (define read (get expr i))
    (if (and (equal? ' < read) (not found))
      ((set! nested (+ 1 nested))
       (if (equal? nested 1)
         ((set! before accum)
          (set! accum nil))
         (set accum (push accum read))))
      (if (and (equal? ' > read) (not found))
        ((set! nested (- 1 nested))
         (if (equal? nested 0)
           ((set! found #t)
            (set! paren (parse accum))
            (set! accum nil))
           (set accum (push accum read))))
        (set accum (push accum read))))))
  (if paren
    (concat (push before paren) (parse accum))
    expr)))
```

Figure 4.21:

```
(define funparse (lambda
   (expr nested before paren accum found)
   (if (null? expr)
      (if (not (null? paren))
         (concat (push before paren) (funparse_ accum))
         expr)
      ((let read (get expr 0)
         (if (and (equal? read ' <) (not found)))
            ((set! nested (+ 1 nested))
             (if (equal? 1 nested)
                ((set! before accum)
                 (set! accum nil))
                (set accum (push accum read))))
         (if (and (equal? read ' >) (not found)))
            ((set! nested (- 1 nested))
             (if (equal? 0 nested)
                ((set! paren (funparse_ accum))
                 (set! found #t)
               (set! accum nil))
                (set accum (push accum read))))
         (set accum (push accum read)))
      (funparse (cdr expr) nested before paren accum found)))))
(define funparse_ (lambda (expr)
   (funparse expr 0 '() '() '() #f)))
```

We now remove mutation to achieve implementation of the final principle we listed. Our means of achieving this is by allowing all values to be function arguments or expressions operating on arguments.

You should begin to see how our rewrite of this algorithm reads much more as an inductive definition than as a description of a process. In the following section we will make this even more evident.

4.2.8   Adopting a Few Conventions

There are a few vestiges of our initial, imperative implementation which we will now remove. Of note is the prior *define* keyword that was appropriately substituted by *letrec*, with *funparse_* then being another definition within the *letrec* procedure.

4.2.9   The Parser

The parser now works as in Figure 4.24.

4.2.10   Evaluation

Combining the prior evaluator with the new addition of the parser, we have the behavior you would have expected.

Figure 4.22:

```
(define funparse (lambda (expr nested before paren accum found)
   (if (null? expr)
     (if (not (null? paren))
        (concat (push before paren) (funparse_ accum))
        expr)
     (if (and (equal? ' < (get expr 0)) (not found))
        (if (equal? nested 0)
          (funparse
        (cdr expr) (+ nested 1)
        accum paren
        nil found)
          (funparse
        (cdr expr) (+ nested 1)
        before paren
        (push accum (car expr)) found))
        (if (and (equal? ' > (get expr 0)) (not found))
          (if (equal? nested 1)
            (funparse
        (cdr expr) (− nested 1)
        before (funparse_ accum)
        nil #t)
            (funparse
        (cdr expr) (− nested 1)
        before paren
        (push accum (car expr)) found))
          (funparse
        (cdr expr) nested
        before paren
        (push accum (car expr)) found))))))
(define funparse_ (lambda (expr)
   (funparse expr 0 '() '() '() #f)))
```

Figure 4.23:

(letrec funparse (lambda (funparse expr nested before paren accum found)
  (let
    *funparse_*
    (lambda (expr) (funparse expr 0 '() '() '() #f))
    (if (null? expr)
      (if (null? paren)
        expr
        (concat (push before paren) (funparse_ accum)))
      (if (and (equal? ' < (car expr)) (not found))
        (if (equal? nested 0)
          (funparse
        (cdr expr) (+ nested 1)
        accum paren
        nil found)
          (funparse
        (cdr expr) (+ nested 1)
        before paren
        (push accum (car expr)) found))
        (if (and (equal? ' > (car expr)) (not found))
          (if (equal? nested 1)
            (funparse
          (cdr expr) (− nested 1)
          before (funparse_ accum)
          nil #t)
            (funparse
          (cdr expr) (− nested 1)
          before paren
          (push accum (car expr)) found))
          (funparse
        (cdr expr) nested
        before paren
        (push accum (car expr)) found)))))) ...)

Figure 4.24:

$(letrec\, parse\, (lambda\, (\dots)\, \dots)$
$\quad (parse\, '(< a > < b < c > > < d >)))$
$\implies\ ((a)\, (b\, (c))\, (d))$

Chapter 5

A Self-Hosted Language

In the previous section, we successfully designed and implemented an interpreter of the Lambda Calculus. This was a very interesting problem to solve, because it allowed us to form a grammar of expression from within our working language; then allowing us to expand upon this grammar dynamically.

This achievement opens one up to question the limitations of the embedded language. Specifically, we would be concerned with a language sufficiently advanced to form an interpreter of itself, and to then add features.

This phenomenon, a sort of singularity, is known in computation as a bootstrapped interpreter. In this section, we will aim to bootstrap our symbolic language, and to then unlock the potential of additional features.

5.1 The Grammar

The grammar of our symbolic language is slightly more complex than the Lambda Calculus; however, it is luckily once again very uniform. However, because we are now defining our grammar within another language, we will need to abstract over the implementation details of token representation. That is to say, although each string is a functional linked-list, we will consider them atomic just as in prior grammar definitions.

We return briefly to our formal definition of a Symbolic Expression from an earlier chapter; this time we will explicate the characters allowed in an *atom*.

Figure 5.1:

< expr >	::= < sexpr > | < atom >
< sexpr >	::= (< list >)
< list >	::= < expr > | < expr > < expr >
< atom >	::= < char > | < atom > < char >
< char >	::= < letter > | < number > | < symbol >
< letter >	::= A | B | ... | Z
< number >	::= 0 | 1 | ... | 9
< symbol >	::= * | + | − | / | # | < | > | _ | ? | !

Now, because we will be operating from within our Symbolic Language, we will be able to abstract away the details of the grammar. That is, S-Expressions will be represented as S-Expressions when provided as input to the interpreter, as will atoms as atoms.

5.2   Self-Interpretaion

5.2.1   Lambda Forms

Recall from our definition of the Symbolic Language in terms of the Lambda Calculus that there were some functions considered more primitive to the language than others. We will expose these to the language which we interpret. Our first task is to enable the Lambda Calculus in these forms, not unlike in our earliest definition of the language.

This is all fine; however, notice that the arguments to the function are evaluated all at once and passed to the an applier-function. In the next section, we will discuss a better approach to evaluation.

5.2.2   Laziness

This is not optimal, and does not allow for some nice features enabled by "laziness" in the interpreter. For this reason, we will

Figure 5.2:

```
(letrec eval (eval expr env)
    (cond (((atom? expr) (assoc expr env))
          ((and
              (atom? (car expr))
              (equal? (car expr) 'lambda))
            (lambda (x)
              (eval
                (caddr expr)
                (set (cadr expr) x env))))
          (#t (apply-set
              (eval (car expr) env)
              (map (lambda (x) (eval x env)) (cdr expr)))))) ...)
```

change the application and variable reference components to reflect a lazy approach to evaluation.

With very few changes we were able to implement this lazy approach. We simply made all arguments wrapped in a lambda before their evaluation, and all variable references then reduce these wrappings when appropriate. These small changes will make a world of difference in the potential of expressiveness in our language.

The most evident of advantages is in the ability to branch execution, i.e., perform *if* statements, without evaluating both branches. This later translates into the ability to recurse without invoking infinite recursion.

5.2.3 Numbers

In order to interpret numbers, we would need our atomic values to be not so atomic. Rather than have atoms go against this nature, we will delay implementation of arbitrary numbers. For now, we will start with single digits.

The code in Figure 5.4 is just another *eval* function, this time appending to the environment a prelude of definitions prior to calling the usual *eval* function. The equivalencies presented are merely

Figure 5.3:

```
(letrec eval (eval expr env)
    (cond (((atom? expr) ((assoc expr env) nil))
          ((and
              (atom? (car expr))
              (equal? (car expr) 'lambda))
            (lambda (x)
              (eval
                (caddr expr)
                (set (cadr expr) x env))))
          (#t (apply-set
              (eval (car expr) env)
              (map
                (lambda (x)
                  (eval (list 'lambda '(  x) env))
                (cdr expr)))))) ...)
```

Figure 5.4:

```
(let eval-prelude (lambda (expr env)
    (eval
      expr
      (concat
        env
        '((0 (0)) (1 (1)) (2 (2)) (3 (3)) (4 (4))
          (5 (5)) (6 (6)) (7 (7)) (8 (8)) (9 (9))))))) ...)
```

from atom to singleton lists; no nature of numbers shows through. Why singletons? Numbers are lists of digits more than they are atomic values, after all, this is what allows us to perform arbitrary arithmetic.

There is one aspect of the environment that we failed to address in our setup of a prelude. Given the lazy nature of our interpreter in which all variable access is reduction of a lambda, we will need to lambda wrap each set value.

Figure 5.5:

```
(let lazy-set (lambda (env hash)
    (concat
        env
        (map (lambda (pair)
            (list
                (car pair)
                (lambda (z) (cadr pair))))
            hash))))
```

The function in Figure 5.5 implements this lazy nature.

It will be our responsibility to implement arithmetic nature of these numbers by means of a *succ* function. As we have already shown, from this definition all else is possible.

The implementation in Figure 5.6 is pretty simple; it is a very basic definition of the meaning of numbers in our decimal system. It says, "One follows zero; two follows one; etc." Next, it communicates the intricacies of place value. A number with a ones digit of nine will increment to a ones digit zero, with a once higher leading strand of digits. Finally, any other number with multiple digits will result in a once larger ones digit.

We will now expand our eval-prelude to be more extensible and to include the *succ* function.

5.2.4 Booleans and Predicates

Our implementation of Booleans will be quite simple. Recall the use of atoms to symbolize numbers in the prior section, with the

Figure 5.6:

```
(let succ (lambda (x)
  (let singles '((0 (1)) (1 (2))
                 (2 (3)) (3 (4))
                 (4 (5)) (5 (6))
                 (6 (7)) (7 (8))
                 (8 (9)) (9 (0 1)))
    (cond (((null? (cdr x)) (assoc singles (car x)))
          ((equal? (car x) 9) (cons 0 (succ (cdr x))))
          (#t (cons (succ (car x)) (cdr x)))))))) ...)
```

Figure 5.7:

```
(let*
  ((set-arithmetic (lambda (env)
     (set
       'succ
       (lambda (x) ...)
       env)))
   (set-numerals (lambda (env)
     (lazy-set
       env
       '((0 (0)) (1 (1)) (2 (2)) (3 (3)) (4 (4))
         (5 (5)) (6 (6)) (7 (7)) (8 (8)) (9 (9)))))))
   (eval-prelude (lambda (expr env)
     (eval
       expr
       (set-arithmetic (set-numerals env)))))) ...)
```

meaning of the numbers being more derived from the operations we defined than from their representation. The same will hold especially true for Booleans.

Our Booleans will be defined on the prelude by the names of t and f, as you have come to expect. Now, rather than decide on an arbitrary atom to which they will map, we will allow f to equal *nil* and t to equal 1. Hence we would have a set-booleans definition to append to *let*∗ that looks like Figure 5.8.

Figure 5.8:

```
(set-booleans (lambda (env)
    (lazy-set env (list (list '#t 1) (list '#f nil))))))
```

Given these definitions of true and false, we will now define an if function which follows very naturally from our native if function.

Figure 5.9:

```
(set-booleans (lambda (env)
    (lazy-set
        env
        (list
            ...
            (list
                'if
                (lambda (p t f)
                    (if (null? x) f t)))))))))
```

5.2.5 List Primitives

The functions primitive to the manipulation of S-Expressions have yet to be discussed. The following is a list of these primitives.

- *car*

- *cdr*

- *cons*

- *eq?*

- *null?*

- *atom?*

These will be exposed to the interpreted language by means of the prelude.

Figure 5.10:

(set-primitives (*lambda* (*env*)
    (lazy-set
      env
      (*list*
        (*list 'car car*)
        (*list 'cdr cdr*)
        (*list 'cons cons*)
        (*list 'eq? equal?*)
        (*list 'null? null?*)
        (*list 'atom? atom?*)))))

5.2.6   Recursion

Now, as was alluded to earlier, we will provide a Y combinator for the sake of recursion. Thanks to the lazy evaluation of our interpreter, this will be an easily achieved task.

Although combinators are possible without lazy evaluation, a function-based *if* statement is not; this is the key to our dependence on laziness. In Figure 5.11, we set a Y-Combinator on the prelude.

Figure 5.11:

(set-Y (*lambda* (*env*)
  (lazy-set
    env
    (*list* (*list* 'Y (*lambda* (*f*)
      ((*lambda* (*x*) (*f* (*x* *x*)))
      (*lambda* (*x*) (*f* (*x* *x*)))))))))))

5.2.7   Syntactic Sugars

In our definition of the language, we were sure to provide convenient shorthands and general niceties. Hence, we will now do the same within our interpreter.

Most of the syntactic constructs which we have yet to address are forms of *let*. For this reason, we begin with an exposure of *let* to the interpreter. *let* is merely syntactic sugar for reduction of a lambda; hence we provide the implementation of let-forms seen in Figure 5.12.

Note that this definition performs a rewrite of the S-Expression, and then evaluates that new form. This is often referred to as a *macro*. Macros can be exposed to the programmer of a language to allow for this same extensibility of the language from *within* the language.

Returning to our syntactic constructs, we similarly define *let*∗ forms. However, in this case, we will extract a function called let-set to avoid messiness in our main interpreter definition.

let-set is recursively defined, but its implementation is very similar to that of *let*. If there are definitions to be applied, let-set creates a wrapping lambda and reduces it with the first definition. Then, it recurses until there are no more definitions to apply. At that time, it returns the expression.

Now, our last let-form is *letrec*. This syntax will be defined using the Y- combinator, as alluded to earlier.

Once again we utilized a macro in our definition of a form; this time simply applying the Y-Combinator prior to execution of *let*.

Figure 5.12:

```
(letrec eval (eval expr env)
  (cond (((atom? expr) ((assoc expr env) nil))
        ((equal? (car expr) 'lambda)
         (lambda (x)
           (eval
             (caddr expr)
             (set (cadr expr) x env))))
        ((equal? (car expr) 'let)
         (eval
           (list
             (list
               'lambda
               (cadr expr)
               (cadddr expr))
             (caddr expr)) env))
        (#t (apply-set
             (eval (car expr) env)
             (map
               (lambda (x)
                 (eval (list 'lambda '() x) env))
               (cdr expr)))))) ... )
```

Figure 5.13:

```
(letrec let-set
   (lambda (let-set defs expr)
     (if
       (null? defs)
       expr
       (list
         (list
           'lambda
           (caar defs)
           (let-set (cdr defs) expr))
         (cadar defs)))))
   (letrec eval (eval expr env)
     (cond (...
             ((equal? (car expr) 'let*)
              (eval (let-set (cadr expr) (caddr expr)) env))
             (#t ...))) ...))
```

Figure 5.14:

```
(letrec eval (eval expr env)
    (cond (...
                ((equal? (car expr) 'letrec)
                 (eval
                    (list
                       'let
                       (cadr expr)
                       (list 'Y (caddr expr))
                       (cadddr expr))
                    env))
                (#t ...))) ...)
```

5.2.8   The Evaluator

The full evaluator is displayed in Figure 5.15 on page 91.

5.2.9   Conclusion

We have successfully defined an interpreter of the syntax of our
language. Even more interesting is the fact that we implemented
this interpreter from within the same language. By taking this
route, we were able to reuse, or *snarf*, some of the constructs of the
language very easily in our interpretation of it.

5.3   Language Expansion

Having successfully allowed our language to interpret itself, we are
now able to take it even farther. That is, we can begin to add
features to our language from within the language itself.

You have probably begun to notice the complexity of some of
our procedures. The nesting of definitions, amongst other things,
leads to an expression very hard for a human reader to parse. Additionally, you might recall from an earlier section the utilization
of mutation in a procedure, attributed to an imperative approach,

Figure 5.15:

```
(letrec let-set
   (lambda (let-set defs expr)
      (...))
   (letrec apply-set
      (lambda (apply-set fn args)
         (...))
      (letrec eval (lambda (eval expr env)
            ...
         (let * ((lazy-set (lambda (env hash)
                     (...)))
               ...
               (eval-prelude (lambda (expr env)
                  (eval
                  expr
                  (set-arithmetic
                        ...
                     (set-Y env))))))))))
         (...))))))
```

as an alternative to this heavy nesting.

In this section, we will implement the beginnings of an array of mutators allowing for the imperative model. We will begin with a single, *set* function without scope. This means that the only way this form will take effect is through its invocation at the top level.

5.3.1   Mathematical Background

An important idea in functional programming is that of the Monad. Its name comes from its origins in Mathematics, more specifically Category Theory. Monad refers to its ability to generate everything from a single value. We, however, will be viewing the Monad in a slightly different light. A Monad is a triple, consisting of a Functor, and two transformations, ν and μ. We will take a moment to unwrap this definition.

A Functor is a construct at a very high level of abstraction, we will briefly define it in terms of familiar concepts. We begin with the idea of a set and a relation on that same set. Of course, an example would be the set of Natural Numbers. Then a relation on that set could be $<$. This will be our first level of abstraction; that is to say, this is our first example of objects and arrows between them. An arrow could flow from 0 to 1, and then 1 to 2, et cetera, ad infinitum.

Given a set and a relation on that set, we will consider the two an object. An object could have multiple relations defined upon it as well. Now, we imagine having two objects, each with a different set and an analogous relation. For example, we might introduce the rational numbers and their ordering. We then call some function from the Natural Number object to the Rational Number object a morphism so long as it preserves the ordering when mapping values from the naturals to the rationals.

Next, we consider a category to be any collection of objects and arrows between those objects. More specifically, a category consists of objects, morphisms between those objects, and compositions of those morphisms.

Finally, we consider a Functor to consist of a mapping of objects and morphisms from one category to another. Returning to our initial prompt, we consider a monad to be a map from one category to another, along with two transformations.

5.3.2 Monads in Computation

Given the previous explanation of Monads, it is probably still unclear how the structure would relate to computation. We will now take a look at the traits of the transformations ν and μ. Let T refer to the Functor of a given Monad. The transformation ν then yields ν_x such that ν_x is a function from x to $T(x)$. Similarly, the transformation μ yields μ_x such that μ_x is a function from $T(T(x))$ to $T(x)$. Thus, we can see that a Monad includes a way of adding and taking away mappings by the Functor. If we consider a map by the Functor to be a boxing of the value, we have that ν_x boxes members of x, and that μ_x unboxes a box of boxes. In a similar vein, we will refer to ν as unit and μ as join.

Now, one might be wondering why such a structure is valuable. The reason is that Monads generalize the idea of boxing values. Why box values? One might box a value in a pair, with an annotation as the other element. For example, one could define a couting Monad which boxes by forming a tuple including the value and 1 and unboxes a box of a box by adding together the number labels as follows.

Figure 5.16:

$$
\begin{aligned}
T(x) &= x \times \mathbb{N} \\
T(f : A \to B)(a, n) &= (f(a), n) \\
\nu_x : x &\to T(x) \\
\nu_x(x) &= (x, 1) \\
\mu_x : T(T(x)) &\to T(x) \\
\mu_x((x, a), b) &= (x, a + b)
\end{aligned}
$$

A similar construct, then, could be used to accumulate log information, for example. Monads are of interest to us for their potential in maintaining state. For this purpose, one could maintain state as the second element of the tuple. However, for applications like this one, programmers usually prefer to take a different outlook on Monads, namely, to focus on *unit* and *bind* functions rather than *unit* and *join*. The bind function can be defined in terms of join quite simply.

As you can see in Figure 5.17, *bind* essentially elevates a func-

Figure 5.17:

$$bind_x : T(A) \rightarrow (A \rightarrow T(B)) \rightarrow T(B)$$
$$bind_x(a,\ f) \ = \ join(T(f)(a))$$

tion from unboxed to boxed to boxed to boxed. Its innerworkings are as simple as getting the boxed morphism defined by the category which accepts a function from A to $T(B)$ and returns a function from $T(A)$ to $T(T(B))$. However, since we are seeking a function onto $T(B)$, we then unbox the return value with *join*.

5.3.3   A New Eval

In our new eval function we will form a function which boxes our previous implementation with an environment. However, we will implement the unboxing and boxing by hand in a full rewrite, to drive home the innerworkings of it.

The code in Figure 5.18 is a rewrite of the *eval* function to behave as this composite form. Note that macro forms behave the same as before, but that all other forms return a list of expression result and environment. Of course, these forms are also forced to interface with the new return values of *eval* in order to bear the same effect as before.

With this new eval function, we have a way of maintaining state after mutation to the environment. Now we can define a function which will accept a list of expressions and perform them one after the other on a gradually mutating environment.

Hence we would achieve the behavior exhibited by the Figure 5.20.

5.3.4   Scope

So far we have for the most part left the environment alone, excepting for invocations of *set!*. However, we will now take a look at scope and how it will be implemented through the various syntactic forms.

The first prerequisite will be the existence of various scopes in which a variable may be defined. For these to be present, we will

Figure 5.18:

```
(letrec eval (eval expr env)
  (cond (((atom? expr) (list ((assoc expr env) nil) env))
        ((equal? (car expr) 'lambda)
         (list
           (lambda (x)
             (eval
               (caddr expr)
               (set (cadr expr) x env)))
           env)
        ((equal? (car expr) 'let)
         (...))
        ((equal? (car expr) 'letrec)
         (...))
        ((equal? (car expr) 'let*)
         (...))
        ((equal? (car expr) 'set!)
         (list
           #t
           (set
             (cadr expr)
             (car (eval (caddr expr) env))
             env)))
        (#t (list
               (car (apply-set
                 (car (eval (car expr) env))
                 (map
                   (lambda (x)
                     (car (eval (list 'lambda '() x) env)) (cdr expr)))))
               env)))) ...)
```

Figure 5.19:

(*letrec* eval-seq (*lambda* (eval-seq *exprs m*)
   (*if*
      (*null? exprs*)
      m
      (eval-seq (*cdr exprs*) (*eval* (*car exprs*) (*cadr m*))))))

Figure 5.20:

(*car* (eval-seq ′((*set! c* 1) (*c*)))) ⟹ 1

need sub-procedures with their own environments; that is, we will
need lambdas with bodies of multiple expressions.

Implementation of this feature is far from difficult. We may as
well embrace our early stages of an expanded language and provide as a prelude the eval-seq function. The code in Figure 5.21
combines our set function with the Y-Combinator to form an alternative to let-rec. Note that we have modified the function definition to return the full value-environment pair, rather than just
the value.

Figure 5.21:

(*set!* eval-seq (*Y* (*lambda* (eval-seq *exprs m*)
   (*if*
      (*null? exprs*)
      m
      (eval-seq (*cdr exprs*) (*eval* (*car exprs*) (*cadr m*)))))))

Now we can utilize eval-seq from within the *eval* function; we
will call it from within the evaluation of a lambda.

Figure 5.22:

```
(set! eval-lambda (lambda (eval expr env)
  (list
    (lambda (x)
      (eval-seq
        (cddr expr)
        (list
          #t
          (set (cadr expr) x env)))
      env))
```

Note our use of *cddr* rather than *caddr*. This is the portion of the implementation accounting for a sequence of expressions following the parameter list of a lambda definition. Additionally, notice that the initial environment had to account for the full form expected by eval-seq, i.e., a value-environment pair.

What are the ramifications of this straightforward foundation for scope? Our use of eval-seq sufficed for maintenance of values in the sequence of lambda body-expressions; however, it served to form a sort of fork from the primary environment, one which never reconnects with its origin. We are now faced with the problem of implementing this scope-traversal despite the current forking.

In order to achieve this, we have already decided that a scope-traversing function will be required. How would one be implemented? Well, if you attempt to find the point at which two environments share a border, it is clearly at the forming of a lambda. Hence, we could define a function, say bubble-set!, on the lambda's environment which will set a value on the parent environment if the variable has yet to be declared on the child.

There is one issue with this idea, however: the environment value is not mutable. Hence, we cannot simply change a value on it. Rather, we will need to perform a manipulation at the return-time of the environment. To achieve this, we will need to modify the default clause of the evaluator: application. The code in Figure 5.23 would take on the environment value of the forked environment.

This is not suitable, because you would then have all ideas of

Figure 5.23:

```
(#t (apply-set
        (car (eval (car expr) env))
        (map
          (lambda (x)
            (car (eval (list 'lambda '( ) x) env)) (cdr expr)))))))
```

scope be lost to a system of most recently set values. Instead, we will need to harness the forked environment for manipulations on the primary environment, and then discard it. The definition of perform-bubbles in Figure 5.24 handles the updating of the primary environment.

Of special note is the fact that rather than perform the value updates on the environment manually, we allowed the evaluator to perform them. This choice will prove helpful later when we devise a more formal scoping system governed by rules based on variable declaration.

We are now left only with the issue of simulating updates to the primary environment from within the forked environment. This can be achieved by some tweaks to variable access and setting.

The two definitions in Figure 5.25 serve to attempt either a get or set on the forked environment, and, if the variable is undeclared, perform that action on the *bubble* portion of the environment. Of course, when appropriate, these bubbles will be reflected in the primary environment.

Despite the elegance of the earlier definitions, our current foundation will not allow them to be effective. Currently, we are creating the forked environment from the primary environment. This means that changes to the primary environment will not be seen as needing to bubble, but rather, as changes to local variables. To resolve this issue, we will need to change our initial value for forked environments.

The code in Figure 5.26 is quite simple. Our only change was to specify the primary environment as the bubbling cache.

You may have picked up on the fact that since all set operations bubble if the variable is undeclared, *set*! will not suffice if we wish to maintain various scopes. For this purpose, we will introduce a

Figure 5.24:

```
(set! perform-bubbles (lambda (m env)
   (let bubbles (assoc 'bubbles (cadr m))
     (list
        (car m)
        (cadr
           (eval-seq
              (map (lambda (b) (cons 'set! b)) bubbles)
              m))))))
...
(#t (perform-bubbles (apply-set
        (car (eval (car expr) env))
        (map
           (lambda (x)
              (car (eval (list 'lambda '() x) env)) (cdr expr)))))) env))
```

Figure 5.25:

```
((atom? expr)
  (if
    (present? expr env)
    (list ((assoc expr env) nil) env)
    (list ((assoc expr (assoc 'bubble env)) nil) env)))
...
((equal? (car expr) 'set!)
(list
  #t
  (if
    (present? expr env)
    (set
      (cadr expr)
      (eval (caddr expr) env)
      env)
    (set
      'bubble
      (set
        (cadr expr)
        (eval (caddr expr) env)
        (assoc 'bubble env))
      env)))))
```

Figure 5.26:

```
(set! eval-lambda (lambda (eval expr env)
  (list
    (lambda (x)
      (eval-seq
        (cddr expr)
        (list
          #t
          (set (cadr expr) x '((bubble env)))))))
  env))
```

define function. *define* will pin down a variable to a specific scope, if you will. Its implementation is merely a reuse of our original, naive set function.

Figure 5.27:

```
((equal? (car expr) 'define)
  (list
    #t
    (set
      (cadr expr)
      (eval (caddr expr) env)
      env)))
```

Together, *define* and *set!* provide us with the ability to specify scope for variables which will be maintained across any sort of sub-procedure. Our implementation of a bubbling *set!* was very slick, and *define* was merely a reuse of our old *set!* function.

5.4   Conclusion

We have defined a means of evaluating our language from within
the language itself.   Once this was done, we were able to expand upon the language's constructs, adding imperative features,
amongst other features. This is not merely an academic exercise,
but the way in which programming languages have evolved from
the time of the first computers. Henceforth, the grammar of our
language will be dynamic and fully extensible.

www.ingramcontent.com/pod-product-compliance
Lightning Source LLC
Chambersburg PA
CBHW022108170526
45157CB00004B/1538